Friedhelm Schwarz

Creating Shared Value

Peter Brabeck-Letmathe
and Nestlé – a Portrait

Friedhelm Schwarz

Creating Shared Value

Peter Brabeck-Letmathe and Nestlé – a Portrait

Stämpfli Verlag AG

The bibliographical information in the German National Bibliography can be found on www.d-nb.de

Editors · Esther Hürlimann, Zürich
Translation · TransNation Translations, Inc.
Typography · Satzart AG, Bern
Cover Design · Nils Hertig, clicdesign ag, Liebefeld
Printing · fgb • freiburger graphische betriebe, Freiburg

ISBN 978-3-7272-1290-1

Printed in Germany

Table of Contents

Foreword by Klaus Schwab

This portrait of Peter Brabeck-Letmathe is quite different from what one normally associates with biographies. It is neither a mere chronological account of a life, nor a retrospective of a life's work now completed. The person who is the subject of this book, Peter Brabeck, is still looking forward, open to new ideas; he is analytical and provides others with food for thought, changing and moving things just as he has always done. And that is exactly what this book clearly illustrates.

The author does not analyze and interpret the man who is Brabeck in order to draw attention to himself and his own point of view, but rather collects and organizes facts and anecdotes, thereby creating a portrait of an accomplished man who thinks and acts in complex ways. The author refrains from superfluous commentary, because the story speaks for itself. The reader is offered no prefabricated opinion, but rather the chance to form his own.

This is accomplished, largely through the use of numerous interviews and conversations with interesting leading personalities who know Peter Brabeck well and portray him from their own varied perspectives.

Among the special features of this book is the prologue written by Peter Brabeck-Letmathe himself, in which he connects his December 2008 experience on Aconcagua in the Argentine Andes to the ideas which are important to him, in an impressive way.

Many different aspects open up for the reader, who comes to know an exceptional human being, and also something about the inner structures and thought processes within one of the greatest and most influential enterprises in the world.

Moreover, the book describes an economic model which proves, in practical terms, that everyone can be a winner and there is no need for anyone to lose out. This principle of Creating Shared Value is what raises Peter Brabeck-Letmathe, and Nestlé itself, above many other successful business leaders and companies. The contribution of Switzerland and its inherent values to this is not overlooked. Taking on responsibilities with a long-term perspective and being accountable for one's actions are economic virtues which cannot be valued highly enough in the present day.

Prof. Klaus Schwab
World Economic Forum
Geneva, November 2009

Prologue by Peter Brabeck-Letmathe

Saturday, 20 December 2008, Mendoza

The flight from Miami to Santiago and then over the Andes offered me two wonderful views of the mountain which I've marveled at so many times since the first time I came to Chile in August 1970, but which, until now, was not on my list of peaks to conquer. Aconcagua, at 6,962 meters above sea level, is not only the tallest mountain in the Americas, but also the highest peak outside Asia.

The view from the plane offers the best opportunity to take it all in: the impressive glacial South Face, thousands of meters high, which would present a technical and personal challenge to even the best mountaineer, and the Northwest Face, the normal route, with its path winding its way through a 38-kilometer long valley to base camp, before leading over boulders, stones, rocks and ice up to the peak. But what the two sides have in common is their height – and, above all, the fact that they are both at the mercy of the wind and extreme weather conditions. To the west of the mountain lies the Pacific Ocean and to the east the Argentine Pampas, with the result that two different climates collide over the mountain, leading to very sudden and radical weather changes – something which I would later experience for myself.

The plane was already beginning its descent and in a few minutes would be landing in Mendoza where my adventure begins – although not as it had been originally planned.

A few months earlier, I'd run into a skiing friend during a business flight to New York – a private banker from Geneva, who had decided to climb Aconcagua for his sixtieth birthday. He convinced me to accompany him. And so everything was planned. I was already scheduled to be in New York again on business in mid-December, after which I would fly directly on to South America, sending my mountaineering pack ahead of me. Then, in New York, I received a phone call: "You've probably already got wind of the Madoff scandal. I'm going to have to stay near my clients in order to represent their interests. I'm afraid I have to cancel on you."

I was incredibly disappointed. I had prepared myself physically for the expedition and my pack was already there. Finally I decided to phone a friend in Chile who had once told me about an expedition tour operator there and asked him to arrange a mountain guide and the climbing logistics for me.

Just twenty-four hours later I received word that it was all organized; I would be picked up at the airport in Mendoza on the 20th of December.

Everything went as planned: the Company, "Vertical," from Santiago de Chile, had sent two young mountain guides and my pack to Mendoza to help me with the authorization permit paperwork and to do a final check of the expedition equipment.

We spent the day packing everything so it could be carried by the mules. An evening in the garden of an excellent Grill was devoted to mountaineering stories and anecdotes, and to me trying to learn as much as I could from my two mountain guides about their experiences on Aconcagua. My excitement was growing; the long overnight flight and the thought of the intensive upcoming day couldn't stop us from talking long into the night.

Sunday, 21 December 2008, Mendoza–Confluencia

On the morning of December 21st we were joined by the mountain guide who was to accompany me to the peak: Ernesto Olivares, probably the most famous Chilean mountaineer. He not only knew the Andes from north to south like the back of his hand, but had also climbed some of Asia's eight-thousand meter peaks, including Mount Everest and Nanga Parbat. So I wasn't just in safe hands, but famous ones too. Ernesto Olivares had brought an assistant along, Guillermo Trujillo. He would accompany us and also take part of my pack from me at high altitudes.

The registration and authorization formalities had to be dealt with in person in Mendoza. We got it done in the morning so that we could set off by car towards Aconcagua National Park around midday.

The approach to Penitentes is an experience in itself; the high mineral content of the dry and mostly barren low Andes creates an incredible display of colors.

In Penitentes, we load our packs from the Jeep onto the waiting mules. Before long we're at the entrance to the nature park and begin our ascent to the first camp.

The first few hours of a climb are usually very pleasant and almost easy: green meadows, small lakes, the pack still feels light, conversation with new friends provides entertainment, your body handles the gentle slope without any great effort, and the ultimate goal is so far away that its reality has not yet come into focus.

The late afternoon sun shines above us as we suddenly come upon our first camp, Confluencia, at 3,400 meters. The higher peaks are bathed in glistening light while in the shade of the valley we quickly change into warmer clothes. Tonight will be the first of many cold nights.

Monday, 22 December 2008

Today is important for the acclimatization process. I am convinced that if you want to have enduring success, be it in mountaineering or in the business world, it is essential not to skip any stages.

I feel so good that I feel ready to push on to the base camp at 4,350 meters, but I would pay the price for it later in the critical high altitudes.

A solid foundation is the true prerequisite for enduring success, and nothing in life saves you so much time as truth.

Today we do a comfortable seven-hour trek up to a look-out point at more than 4,000 meters, which offers a spectacular view of the South Face of Aconcagua. Looking across at it, Ernesto tells me stories about the different climbing routes: the first ever ascent, the tragedies and the joys that this mountain has brought the best mountaineers in the world. Lost in thought about how these peaks continue to challenge mankind, as we risk our lives on them, we walk back to base camp in the dusk.

After many years of mountaineering, I am now convinced that a climber is only successful in his mission if he is still healthy when he comes back down to the valley. Of course, reaching the summit is an important motivating factor, but it shouldn't be the only goal. I'm of the opinion that you shouldn't expend 100 percent of your energy in reaching the summit, but only around 80 percent, because you need some energy for the descent as well. The famous "Peter's Principle" of the business world applies here too: for some, the summit can be one step too high and the attempt to reach it will end tragically. The mountain forces us to think in relativistic terms: what is a joyful, easily attained experience for a young, well-prepared mountaineer can be a demanding and serious undertaking for an older man. Or as Reinhold Messner puts it: "The older a mountain climber gets, the higher the mountains."

Tuesday, 23 December 2008

It's not the most demanding day, but it is a challenging one. The distance we have to cover is over 30 kilometers, first down to 3,200 meters then slowly climbing along a huge riverbed, and then a steep section, the Cuesta Brava, to finally reach our base camp at Plaza de Mulas (4,400 meters above sea level) which is also the final stop for the mules.

The sun is high in the sky and there's no shade. There are also plenty of boulders and loose rocks. We trek along in a line and don't speak much: it's a day for reflection and making our way on autopilot.

You find them on all mountain expeditions: the stages that don't demand anything special but nonetheless require stamina, hours of steady trekking. Time to reflect. These stages have often provided the backdrop for my creative entrepreneurial work, when innovative thoughts would spring out of my subconscious or fragments of thoughts would form themselves into new ideas.

Nowadays, we seldom have the time – or indeed, take the time – to think about something for hours, to look at it from the most varied of perspectives, to break it down into its component parts and then reconstruct it afresh, work out new variants and suddenly find ourselves confronted with it in a new form that didn't exist before.

Creative work, even in the business world, certainly doesn't come from an overflow of information and "multimedia exposure," but from the painful work of abstraction, decomposition and reorganization, for which a lot of time and uninterrupted concentration is required. For me personally, the stages of a mountain climb provide me with the opportunity to do this! I believe that making major decisions within a hectic environment is very dangerous. A moment of patience can prevent a lot of misfortune, and being a little more laid back can often show us a better path.

I came to this realization through my mountaineering experience, and I share the opinion of Confucius, who said, "Man has three paths to wisdom: first by reflection which is the noblest; second by imitation which is the easiest, and the third by experience which is the most bitter."

A tent, a meal, and the sunset which shows us the ascent to Aconcagua for the first time in blood-red tones, await us at base camp, along with the packs carried by the mules, which we will have to grapple with tomorrow.

Wednesday, 24 December 2008

The sun reaches our tent late today; the ice on the tent wall doesn't melt until as late as 9:15 a.m.

Christmas Eve is filled with preparations for the next decisive stage of the expedition.

Planning and logistics are now coming to the fore: how many days we need, how many camps we plan to stop at, how many liters of water we will need to get from the snow and ice per person, and how much fuel we will need to do so.

Logistics have always been a decisive part of any venture for me. Often the best strategies fail due to inadequate implementation and logistics. I would even add that what makes the difference in business success is not just having the better strategy but above all the organizational ability to translate these strategies into solid, consistent actions carried out by a motivated, top-achieving team.

The example of the Nestlé model is pertinent here. The model's target of five to six percent organic growth, together with continual profit margin gains, the long-term strategic transformation of a food company into a world class nutrition, health and wellness company, whose organizational restructuring was equivalent to transforming a huge tanker into a flexible attack fleet with common supply units. All would have come to naught and been impossible if Nestlé hadn't also designed and implemented a completely new "logistic." This has now gained worldwide renown as GLOBE (Global Business Excellence). We dedicated 3 billion Swiss francs, 2,100 people and six years' development to it. It is not without good cause that I speak of GLOBE as probably the most important legacy of my term as CEO.

Without GLOBE we would never have been able to make our strategy a reality nor develop the vast competitive advantage that GLOBE still affords us today.

Even on a small expedition, logistical decisions play an important role: every extra unnecessary kilo in a rucksack can cost you a great deal of energy at high altitudes; every kilogram too few can mean not enough energy or vulnerability to the freezing temperatures. Just as the correct balance of working capital in an enterprise can mean the difference between success and failure, the right balance has to be found.

The afternoon passes quickly, spent with the obligatory visit to the doctor and chatting with fellow climbers. After a short, lovingly-prepared Christmas meal, good wishes and thoughts of family, the day comes to an end.

Thursday, 25 December 2008

This morning we all feel good and decide not to make use of the Plaza Canada camp at 5,080 meters, but to carry on and climb directly up to the high altitude camp Nido de Cóndores (5,590 meters above sea level).

It's a long, steep path, but we all take it in our stride. This reminds me of the Chinese saying: "If you want to go quickly, go alone. If you want to go a long distance – go together."

The imagery that enters your mind during a climb could never occur just sitting at home in an armchair.

This slow, continuous ascent up the mountain confronts me head-on with what I often unpleasantly encounter in the business world, above all in the world of finance: the push forward in a blind and overzealous manner, rather than a mature, contemplative approach. I sometimes get the feeling that the finance people of this world live by the motto: "We must be faster, because we are more expensive." But, of course, the reality is different! They ought to be better, because they are more expensive. But that is probably an illusory hope.

Nido de Cóndores is the last plateau, and beyond it you can see the peak stretching up. We arrive by late afternoon and pitch our tents. I lie down in my sleeping bag and watch through the tent opening as my companions melt ice into water.

Running water is the most important resource on the mountain! Actually not only on the mountain, in my opinion water is the most important resource for mankind in general. And despite this, it is not recognized as such nor valued enough. I have dedicated myself wholeheartedly to the water issue for four years now, and it will continue to absorb a great deal of my time.

The higher we climb, the more the view changes. From our camp we can now see many peaks below us that not long ago we had been looking up to in awe. As the lights go on at base camp far below us, we're still sitting up here in the bright evening sunlight.

I watch as my two mountain guides prepare the evening meal in the next tent. They're glowing with contentment; they clearly enjoy being here. To me they embody something I often say to young people who are setting out on their career paths: "Choose a job you love and you'll never have to work a day in your life" (Confucius).

Friday, 26 December 2008

The night was very cold, and I'm looking forward to the first rays of sunlight and hot tea.

We don't have a fixed schedule yet and plan instead to see how I feel at this altitude. We go for a three-hour trek which goes very well, so after lunch we decide to climb up to the next camp Refugio Berlin (approx. 6,000 meters above sea level), and then to attempt the ascent to the summit the next morning.

Once again we pick out the necessary items to take and divide the load, leaving the rest behind in the tent. We set off at 2 pm, in beautiful weather and with a wonderful view of the summit before us.

Just two hours later, we're trudging up the mountain in the midst of an immense snowstorm, but thanks to Ernesto, who has climbed the mountain nine times before this, we manage to find the bivouac shelter in the scheduled time. We set up camp on the now icy ground. The sounds of the storm howling and the gas burner turning the snow into our all-important drinking water fill our ears as we settle into the warmth of our sleeping bags, each of us most likely thinking to himself: what now?

Of course, the decision about our next step lies with the mountain guides, but the opinions and suggestions of every participant in the expedition count. At the end of the day, it's the same up on the mountain as it is down below: It is only individuals who can exercise freedom, develop trust and take on responsibility, not organizations.

As the evening draws on, the wind dies down and at 9 p.m. hours we make the decision to wake up at 1 o'clock in the morning, and to set off around an hour later.

Saturday, 27 December 2008, Mendoza

The night is both long and short. Long, because I can't get to sleep and am now feeling the 6,000 meter altitude for the first time. Short, because four hours after the last light goes out, we are up again. Getting dressed is challenging; it takes more than an hour before we eventually set foot outside.

Darkness, snow, wind and black ice await us, and a cold that is just bearable thanks to being wrapped in insulated clothing from head to toe. We make our way slowly up the first precipice which will lead us to a ridge at an altitude of 6,200 meters We're relatively well protected from the wind and make good progress.

But at the very moment when we reach the ridge, a snowstorm from the other side of the mountain tears across us, causing us to lose our balance. The snow beats against our faces with such force that speaking is impossible. A glance at Ernesto, a sign, and we turn back.

Before day breaks we're back in our sleeping bags, snoozing and relieved to be safe in the shelter of the bivouac.

My thoughts turn to a Brazilian mountaineering couple who reached the summit of Aconcagua a few days earlier with a larger group. The woman over-exerted herself so much that she had no more energy to manage the descent and collapsed, exhausted, on the ground. Her husband stayed with her while the rest of the group made the descent to fetch help for the next day. Both had to spend the night without a bivouac sack or sleeping bag. By the time help came the next day, the husband was dead, and the woman had such severe frostbite on her hands and feet that she had to undergo amputations.

This brings up the question of risk management and responsibility in the wider sense. There can be no success without the risk of failure, no real satisfaction without hard work, and no new opportunities to exploit without criticism, and there can be no real leadership without trust.

It's the constant balancing out of risk factors, the objective assessment of strengths and weaknesses and, at the end of the day, listening to intuition, which leads to the most important decisions in life. And as far as responsibility is concerned, I really think that we often look at this too unilaterally. As Laotse said, "Responsibility is not just for what you do, but also what you don't do."

By ten in the morning the sun is shining brightly and, besides the fact that the mountain has a fresh covering of snow, there is no sign of the stormy weather of the last 20 hours. We use the satellite phone to call the meteorological station in Chile and find out that there's a 24-hour window of good conditions before a disruptive weather front is due to reach the mountain. We swiftly make the decision to stay here and to try again tomorrow morning to reach the summit.

Sunday, 28 December 2008

The third day at 6,000 meters begins early when we get up at around 1 a.m. We can't hear any strong winds and a glance outside reveals a sky twinkling with stars. But the temperature outside is –37° C! We pull on all the clothing we have, no inch of our bodies remains uncovered. Despite all this, the shock of the cold as we set off is still great, making me realize just how much the cold can zap your body of strength.

The climb under the starry sky is beautiful, but the cold quickly penetrates our toes and fingertips and before long I can barely feel mine.

We make relatively good progress, but I am increasingly concerned about the signs of frostbite which have become more pronounced by the time we reach the ridge, where the wind and the icy cold have once again joined forces.

After around three hours, we reach Plaza Independencia at a height of 6,400 meters, and I make the decision to turn back. We are the only ones en route to the summit. The wind and temperature prevent us from stopping to rest. The risk of reaching the summit but not making it back down again feels too great to me at this moment.

Both of my mountain guides immediately agree with my decision and are actually, as they tell me later, relieved. We gave it everything we could, but the mountain wouldn't have us on this particular day – not us nor anyone else.

A few days later some were able to celebrate the beauty of conquering this mountain peak, but sadly, six other mountaineers from Great Britain, Italy and Argentina died on the mountain from exhaustion and frostbite. On the mountain, as in life, the line between success and tragedy is often a very fine one.

Creating Shared Value

The mountain environment, the long lonely nights in the tent and the many silent hours of ascent and descent, always lead me to contemplate how we can shape our own lives, and also that of a company, in such a way as to enable an enduring effect projecting long into the future.

Once again I come back to a realization which has crystallized after many years of reflection: only individuals can exercise freedom, develop trust and take on responsibility, not organizations. From that perspective it is clear that it is the people, the employees, who make up the strength of an enterprise. Therefore the core of management and corporate policy should be employee-based. Without their commitment and personal acceptance of the responsibility for the values and principles of a company there can be no long-term success.

Another important foundation for a company's successful sustainable performance is the continued relevance of its products, brands and services to the consumer. In order for Nestlé to meet its sales targets, we need over a billion consumers all over the world to voluntarily choose our products every day. By investing in our products and brands – which requires, among other things, consistent Innovation and Renovation of the brand image – this relevance can be maintained and strengthened. Our goal is that future generations will see our portfolio as both innovative and familiar. Linked with this is the fact that consumers increasingly have a serious and legitimate interest in the principles and social behavior a company adopts. In the current environment, just keeping in line with the rules is only the bare minimum ethical stance for a company; that alone is simply not adequate.

Thirdly, the economic goals of a business must be organized in such a way that lasting value is created for all of those involved – be it the shareholders, employees, consumers, business partners or national economies. We must create these values together! This can only be achieved if sustainability and long-term goals form the basis of the decision-making process. In this sense, Nestlé doesn't strive for short-term profits at the cost of successful, sustained business development. Nonetheless, we recognize the necessity of making a healthy profit each year to ensure support for the Company from shareholders and financial markets, and most importantly, to finance required investments.

I am convinced that the true strength of a company doesn't lie in the size and strength of its operations but in the power of its principles and goals. Climbing the mountain in the evening sun, I feel happy to have the privilege of working for a human company which has the long-term, sustained creation of shared value as its goal and the guiding principle for its activities – and above all, that my own view of life is in such harmony with that of the Company.

Breakfast at Nestlé

Four weeks after Peter Brabeck's adventure on Aconcagua, he is back again among the very different challenges, obligations and deadlines of his everyday life.

It's 7:00 a.m. in the Swiss city of Davos on this January morning in 2009, and there is as yet no sign of the lively hustle and bustle that will be seen two hours later during the annual meeting of the World Economic Forum. The top people in the business and political world are gathered here for their 39th annual meeting, breaking all records with 2,500 participants on location in the stunning Graubünden Alps.

At that early hour, with its bone-chilling –12° C, there are only a handful of people hurrying through the dark streets to get to the 7:20 a.m. Nestlé breakfast on time. It is not the prospect of culinary delights that roused them from their beds so early – the breakfast is deliberately simple – but the hope of getting exclusive, high-value information at first hand. In addition to the official program, many companies host large evening receptions which are then reported in the society papers, where it is not so much the substance, as seeing and being seen that is important. Other companies also invite people to breakfast meetings; but when it comes to quality, exclusivity, and shaping opinion in the context of the World Economic Forum, the place to breakfast is at Nestlé's.

The eighty hand-picked guests, seated at ten round tables, enjoy Nestlé's healthy breakfast. Anyone not enthusiastic about cereal, yoghurt or chocolate can order something else.

The next food crisis – can it be avoided?

The subject of the January 30, 2009 meeting was "The next food crisis – can it be avoided?" Peter Brabeck, Chairman of the Board of Directors, greeted the record number of participants and briefly introduced the subject. He was followed by seven speakers who gave their brief presentations. Brabeck's introduction can be summarized as follows:

The three great crises of today all begin with the letter F: the much-discussed but unresolved financial crisis; the fuel crisis – i.e., the oil crisis – which in Brabeck's view is somewhat exaggerated because he believes there is enough oil for years to come; and, finally, the food crisis.

The main difference between the financial crisis and the food crisis, according to Brabeck, is that the financial crisis mainly affects people living in comfortable circumstances, while the food crisis primarily afflicts the world's poorest people and therefore deserves more attention than it currently receives.

Brabeck describes the background to the food crisis as follows: in 2008, the number of starving people rose to one billion, proving that the goal of defeating hunger and malnourishment by the end of the millennium is far from having been met; instead of eradicating starvation, we are losing ground. In 2008 alone, the number of people suffering from hunger increased by 40 million, which cannot be ascribed to a drop in agricultural production. On the contrary, 2008 saw the world's largest harvest in the history of mankind; grain production rose by 5.4 percent to 2,245 million tons, yet not enough food was produced to meet the requirements forecast for 2009.

The current problems have their roots in the price trends of basic foodstuffs. The prices of the most important grains are up 70 to 80 percent from 2005. This may not be a problem for people eating pasta in elegant restaurants, but it is for the world's poor.

There is much talk about the deleterious effect of speculation on the raw materials exchanges. "Let me be clear, we at Nestlé are against speculation on basic foodstuffs which are necessities of life for people," stresses Peter Brabeck. He adds that in fact, speculators only anticipate future events. Certain expectations and political miscalculations are thus transformed into market prices, and that simply means that the speculators were perhaps a little better informed than other people.

The decline in agricultural productivity is and will remain an important part of the problem, says Brabeck. Until 1990, agricultural productivity was increasing at a significantly faster rate than the worldwide population, and faster than industrial production. As a result, the price of food and agricultural products decreased by more than 70 percent in the past 30 years. That is one of the main reasons for the temporary improvement of nutrition for many people in the world. Unfortunately, the decline in prices also meant a decline in investor interest in agricultural production.

Brabeck thinks that the increase in productivity has slackened in recent years because of our failure to apply all the technology available, for both political and emotional reasons. One example is the debate in Europe about genetically modified crops.

More bad news is the question of water. For example, until a few years ago, Saudi Arabia exported more than three million tons of wheat a year, but then production was stopped because the high demand for irrigation aroused water shortage fears.

Water is a serious problem when growing vegetables, because everywhere in the world where large areas are planted with cereals, there has been extensive diversion of water which has lowered the water table.

According to Brabeck, the present trend gives the following outlook for the future: by 2025, the amount of cereal production that will be lost in the world is of the same order of magnitude as the 30 percent that is presently produced by the USA and India combined; thus one-third of the world's population will be malnourished.

This trend will be further exacerbated by political decisions in favor of bio-fuels. Ethanol production started modestly, and will rise from about 15 million gallons in 2008 to 25 million in 2017. However, if we look at the political objective of replacing 10 to 20 percent of oil consumption with bio-fuel in subsequent years, the situation looks far worse.

Fuel and food are both measured in calories, and measured in calories, the global energy market today is twenty times the size of the market for food. Therefore, if we want to produce just five percent of our energy from vegetable matter, agricultural production will have to be doubled, and with it the consumption of water. That is impossible.

We are already struggling to feed a world population that will soon reach nine billion, stresses Brabeck. If we take into account the shrinking of water reserves, it becomes clear that something has to change in the way we use water. Otherwise feeding nine billion people will be out of the question. Peter Brabeck sees the following steps as the solution to the problem:

1. We need better infrastructure and supply chains to reduce the loss of food en route from producer to consumer.
2. We must introduce methods to stimulate growth in agricultural productivity. This means a second 'green revolution.'
3. Markets must be opened up and past political mistakes corrected.
4. We must solve the problem of water for agriculture by improved regulation and a clearer concept of price and costs.
5. Bio-fuel policies must be reassessed, including a ban on all production of bio-fuels from food sources.

"The world around water"

The idea behind the Nestlé breakfast in Davos is for the participants to use the presentations to form their views of the world situation. This process in turn generates new themes to be included in the official agenda of future World Economic Forum meetings. This is what happened with regard to the subject of water, which was first addressed at a Nestlé breakfast in 2005.

In 2005, Peter Brabeck put the subject of water on the Forum agenda, not anticipating that the event would be overshadowed by the South Asia tsunami of December 25, 2004. This disaster illustrated the destructive power of water and underlined the subsequent importance of drinking water for survival.

The subject "The world around water" was addressed under three headings:

1. Water from the standpoint of society, international law and politics;
2. The danger of global and local water shortages, and how to respond;
3. Business and industry contributions to solving the water problem.

Peter Brabeck wanted to make the world's opinion- and decision-makers aware of the water problem, which needed to be placed on the agenda as one of the subjects of the highest importance. Brabeck used the-world-around-water.net website to ensure that the contents of the 2005 Nestlé breakfast would not be forgotten.

Peter Brabeck also spoke on this occasion about Nestlé's responsibility. Nestlé's share of water consumption worldwide is 0.005 percent, of which 0.0009 percent goes to bottled water. However, Peter Brabeck stressed, Nestlé's responsibility as a global leading food producer goes well beyond these figures, Nestlé is committed to finding ways to utilize water resources sparingly and sustainably.

Brabeck went on to say that everyone must have access to water, and it must be affordable. What came out of the discussion was that water ought to cost something, since people will waste a product that is free. Furthermore, we need to conserve water in all areas of business and agriculture, and also its quality is of major importance throughout the world. Contaminated water is responsible for illnesses in some 2.3 billion people, and 60 percent of infant mortality is attributable to waterborne infectious and parasitic diseases. "Water is therefore a humanitarian asset and, hence, much more than a raw material for commercial use."

In subsequent years, Peter Brabeck brought up the subject of water with more and more emphasis, but sometimes his demands and proposals fell on deaf ears. Certain politicians, nongovernmental agencies and critics of globalization tried to twist his arguments and use them against him. Peter Brabeck dealt with these critics in a July 2006 interview with the German newspaper "Welt am Sonntag:"

" ***By expressing your opinions on the issue of water management you lived up perfectly to the clichéd image of an insatiable global capitalist. Do you regret that?***
No, I don't regret anything. I just spoke the truth and lived up to my responsibility. We are now using the most important resource in the world in an irresponsible way. Water has no price and, therefore, no value for people. That's dangerous.

I was somewhat misunderstood though: the maximum of 5 liters which the average person drinks every day is not the problem; it is the 5,000 liters of water which a single European consumes indirectly, because those 5,000 liters are used to produce the food he eats.

This issue also surfaces with regard to renewable energy, such as ethanol. The plants needed to produce ethanol consume enormous amounts of water. If these costs were included, alternative energy prices would be much higher and we would have to do some serious thinking about the value of water.

You seem to delight in going against the wind. Do you?
I'm used to it, as a mountain climber as well as a manager. Headwinds cannot turn me around. It's part of our social responsibility to stand up for what we believe, regardless of which way the wind blows.

But other managers keep quiet…
Yes, there are businessmen and CEOs who don't see speaking up as part of their job. But we can't leave every decision to the

politicians. I think we should be getting much more involved, and publicly too. Polite hints in private are not enough. Problems like ensuring all mankind access to water will be one of the major themes of the future. We can't run away from that. ”

In March 2007, Nestlé published its water management report, dealing with water consumption within companies, consumer water supply, and water management in agriculture and within communities.

Nestlé gives three reasons for producing this report. First, as the largest food and drink company in the world, Nestlé must access clean water to produce its high quality products. Second, we wish to document what measures are being taken in food production directly controlled by Nestlé, and how access to clean water can be improved, even apart from our business activity. Third, Nestlé pays attention to interest groups and seeks to find ways to improve access to water for everyone in the world. As the report states: "By working together we can have a positive influence on the use of water resources."

This report did not go unnoticed. The German weekly paper "Die Zeit" used it as an occasion for an interview on the subject of water in April 2007, in which Brabeck among other things said: "Water is critical for Nestlé, because people need so many agricultural products. Let's do the math: 50 liters per day is required by the average European for drinking, washing and personal hygiene, but add to that 6,000 liters more to produce our food. Every calorie obtained from plants requires one liter of water for its production, whereas every calorie from raising livestock needs ten liters. That's where the problem lies."

According to Brabeck, the main problem is that no price has been put on water: "Farmers in southern Spain pay only three percent of the amount paid by households. In California, it's only two percent. In many parts of Italy, farmers pump their water from the ground and that's it; nothing is calculated, nothing is paid for. Farming in Spain is not like in Germany, where the water just falls as rain from heaven; but because its water is practically free, Spain has become Europe's garden state."

When asked if water is a basic human right, he answers: "Yes, it is. But only 25 liters per person per day. Different regulations are needed for the thousands of cubic meters used in private swimming pools or farming. South Africa has implemented such regulations, where every family has a right to 6,000 free liters per month, after which they pay. There's no basic human right to have a full swimming pool."

As for the need to protect agriculture, Brabeck argues: "It's simply incomprehensible that we refuse to touch the privileges of a few million people thereby preventing billions of others from improving their life. Every day, we pay a billion dollars in agricultural subsidies. For these amounts we could fly every cow in Europe around the world first class, and take the bulls along for the ride. That's European agricultural policy for you."

On the subject of the price difference between the bottled water sold by Nestlé and tap water – after all, a liter of Vittel costs about 880 times more than water from the tap – Brabeck says: "To get one liter of potable water from the tap in Europe, you need to purify an average of 300 to 400 liters that will disappear in the shower, toilet, washing machine and car washes. No one is using Vittel to wash their dishes or car."

For every liter of bottled water, Nestlé needs an additional 0.6 liters of water for the packaging, cleaning of the bottling plants, and so on. By contrast, the average soft drink needs three to four liters of water, a liter of beer up to seven, and that's before factoring in the cultivation of the hops and malt. So: "The more bottled water you drink, the more water you save."

Banning bottled water will not solve the problem

By far not all public discussions of water have focused on global problems and the future of the human race. Many only serve economic self-interests, as shown by the "Anti-Bottled Water Campaign" in the USA, also adopted by a Swiss politician.

On June 23, 2008, a majority of 250 US mayors at the Mayoral Conference in Miami voted against the use of bottled water. To protect city tap water, but also for environmental reasons, it was resolved that no more mineral water should be bought with money from taxes. Cities in the United States have to spend about 70 million dollars disposing of water bottles, because no European-style deposit or recycling system exists. Even Jacques Neirynck, Christian-Democratic Party member for Vaud in the Swiss national parliament, and honorary professor of the Swiss Federal Institute of Technology (EPFL) in Lausanne, would like to see bottled water sales banned. In his view, bottled water should only be available in pharmacies by prescription. His main argument is to save energy. He maintains that, unlike tap water, the energy costs for filling, transporting and manufacturing the bottles are too high; and it bothers him that much of it is in his view, pure marketing.

Peter Brabeck vehemently opposes such arguments: "Bottled water uses a minimal amount of water and gives the consumer a better quality drink." He added that for political reasons the price of tap water is set too low, therefore there is not enough investment in water pipelines.

In Europe, about 30 percent and in developing countries up to 70 percent of potable water is lost through leaks in water pipes; in Europe only 9 liters of potable water are needed per person per day, but waterworks process 400 liters per person per day.

When we take into account the energy used by the waterworks to purify drinking water that is actually consumed, and the additional costs for replacing and maintaining water infrastructure, the energy price per liter of tap water consumed will be found to be significantly higher than for mineral water.

Brabeck points out that specific brands of bottled water, like other branded products, mean something special to the consumer; otherwise we would find only no name products in supermarkets. Even a century ago, doctors and scientists acknowledged the specific properties and, in certain cases, even the therapeutic value of water from particular sources such as Vittel, Contrex and Perrier, and consumers wanted these products available, since not everyone can afford to go to a spa. As regards environmental protection, Brabeck is convinced that the answer is an efficient recycling program such as in Switzerland.

In 2008, water became a principal subject at the World Economic Summit. As part of the preparations, the founder and the Chairman of the World Economic Forum, Professor Klaus Schwab published a manifesto, co-authored by Peter Brabeck, which was covered in more than 30 media internationally.

The WEF introduced the World Economic Forum Water Initiative as a component of Public-Private Partnership efforts, which concentrated on the themes of "the use of water in agriculture" and "water policy reform." The Forum's efforts are in support of the UN Global Compact's CEO Water Mandate initiative.

At the 2009 World Economic Forum, the subject of water was again on the agenda. Over the years, the WEF has become increasingly important to Peter Brabeck as a platform for his socio-political activities.

As a member of the Board of Trustees and current Chairman of the WEF International Business Council, he found a stage to bring Nestlé into the limelight worldwide.

A global corporate statesman with a real commitment – Conversation with Klaus Schwab

Klaus Schwab, born 1938, studied mechanical engineering in Zurich and graduated as a Doctor of Technical Sciences. He then studied Business Administration in Fribourg, graduating as a Doctor of Economic Science; he then attended Harvard where he was awarded a Master of Public Administration degree. From 1971 to 2002, he was professor of entrepreneurial policies at Geneva University. In 1971, he founded the charitable foundation, European Management Forum, and as Chairman built it into a global communications platform for economic, social and political affairs. In 1987, it was renamed the World Economic Forum. In addition, Schwab founded the non-profit Schwab Foundation for Social Entrepreneurship.

He has retired from all his commercial directorships and consultancies and only sits on committees engaged in cultural or social affairs.

“ ***In what context did you first meet Peter Brabeck? How did you get to know him better since then?***

I've known him for almost twenty years. I first met him when we organized a meeting with Venezuelan Ministers here in Geneva in 1990. He was motivated to come along by his strong interest in South America.

First, I should say a few words about who we are. The World Economic Forum is a membership organization and we're very selective in choosing our members. We limit our number to one thousand and Nestlé has been a member for over twenty years. We have different membership categories and Nestlé has been in the highest level for years. We call them strategic partners, companies with whom we work especially closely, who do more than just participate in our regular activities; we discuss political and economic problems with them, in order to exercise our own function as a bridging organization between the economy and politics.

In 1996 we were very involved in strengthening the links between Eastern and Western Europe and led many high-level discussions in which Peter Brabeck also took part. At the time, Helmut Maucher was Nestlé's top man, but he stepped down as Chairman of the Board in 2000. Thereafter, Peter Brabeck has attended every Davos meeting as Nestlé's top representative.

We think it is important to cultivate close relationships with the biggest companies in the area. That's why Nestlé has been represented on our Board of Trustees for over twenty years, and now Peter Brabeck has taken Helmut Maucher's place as member of the Board.

The composition of our Board of Trustees is probably unlike any other. We are all very committed; we have four meetings a year and always have a turnout of at least 70 percent of the members.

The Board plays a very important role, and Peter Brabeck holds a special position within it. If he disagrees with something or thinks it questionable, he speaks up immediately. He is the most critical member of the Board, but at the same time he is the one I turn to first when a problem comes up.

That says a great deal about his personality. It's not just his willingness to help, but his loyalty. It's also a bond of friendship, a true partnership, that does not rule out even 'unpleasant transparency.' This means we speak our minds, even if it's disagreeable to the other person. That way you always know where you stand. It's not about criticizing someone, but showing that something is important to you and that you are genuinely committed to it.

It's completely natural for strong personalities to have different opinions at times, which you have to deal with. That may be unpleasant at the time, but in the long run you realize that you can rely on them absolutely. That's what I especially like about Peter Brabeck.

At the same time, he is loyal, and doesn't bear a grudge if you don't follow his advice. He's done his duty by expressing his opinion, and if I, as happened more than once, made a different decision, he never held it against me. I don't mean to imply that our relationship is characterized by differences of opinion, but when they did arise, it was usually because he is an entrepreneur, which gives him a different perspective.

Peter Brabeck is more risk-conscious than I am. His policies as an entrepreneur were always shaped by the fact that he is very cautious but also persistent. You can see this from the way he transformed Nestlé from a traditional food manufacturer into an enterprise for healthy, modern nutrition. He did this by taking small, and sometimes much bigger steps without neglecting tried-and-true traditions.

Because at the Forum, we aim to reflect the swiftly changing world, Peter Brabeck sometimes thought we were active in too many areas, thereby putting quality at risk. However, our success so far has proved that we are on the right track.

We are not a company, but a not-for-profit foundation that is nonetheless driven by an entrepreneurial spirit. Despite the financial crisis, we experienced a growth of 15 percent in the 2008-9 fiscal year, and exceeded our expectations in all areas. The number of participants and our waiting lists have set new records in all membership categories.

You asked me how I got to know Mr. Brabeck better. Let me tell you a story about that. I had been aware of him for a number of years as a member of the Nestlé leadership team, but never got to know him personally. That changed in January of 2002 when we decided to move our annual meeting from Davos to New York, to show solidarity with our American members after 9/11.

I had invited leading Islamic, Jewish and Christian religious representatives to this meeting in New York. On a very cold morning in January, I went with them to Ground Zero, the former site of the World Trade Center, where we planned to hold a small memorial service. We didn't tell the other participants about it. As we were sitting in the bus, I suddenly saw that Mr. Brabeck was there too. He had heard about it and was determined to come along.

For the first time, I saw him from a very human, personal perspective. The different religious representatives said their prayers. It was very moving and most of them had tears in their eyes. I saw that Mr. Brabeck was also emotionally moved.

At that moment I felt a bond with him. It is often very difficult to show your truly human side, when, like Mr. Brabeck, you are in a demanding leadership position, you are always needed somewhere and every minute of your time is planned.

That trip to the ruins of the Twin Towers and our inter-faith memorial service for the victims really shaped my relationship with him. We were only a small group and it created a bond between us.

There is one more thing which I have in common with Mr. Brabeck. I believe that someone in a leadership role should be physically fit and not lose their connection to nature. For me it is very important to climb a 4,000-meter mountain two to three times a year, although sometimes I only manage to get out once. I go with my colleagues from the Forum, usually around thirty of us, to Gran Paradiso, Mont Blanc or Monte Rosa. Each year we climb one of the big peaks.

Intense expeditions like these are very important to me for a number of reasons. First, because it shows you whether you're physically fit, even at sixty or in my case, even older. Second, because you are part of a team, and everyone in the team is equal, whether you're in a lodge sharing a dormitory with thirty other people or in a tent, you're all sharing the same destiny; you are one of many, part of a team.

I know that Mr. Brabeck as a mountaineer shares this same philosophy. This shows me that despite the aloofness of the business world, he has no problem coming down to the grassroots level.

It is also important for him to keep his private life separate from his professional life. He doesn't look for social opportunities to put himself in the limelight. This has always impressed me a great deal. With the exception of concerts in Salzburg or Lucerne, I've never seen him at a social event.

His ties to music and nature, and keeping his family and his work separate, give Peter Brabeck a deeply human dimension and have kept him from being too aloof. He always comes across as someone who has stayed true to himself, with a clear, naturally evolved identity, not manipulated by PR people.

It appears that his success lies in the fact that he is both an outstanding leader and a genuine human being. For me, three things make a leader: first, a leader needs a clear vision. Second, this vision should go beyond dreams and be transformed into strategies. And third, he or she should be capable of implementing these strategies.

Many lack vision, or they have vision and can formulate strategies but can't translate this into action. Peter Brabeck, clearly has firmly developed all three of these attributes. This gives him the strength to lead, which goes beyond the professional side. It also involves a system of values.

I know many of the world's great personalities. Peter Brabeck is one of the ten people in the world who have made the biggest impression on me, together with figures such as Nelson Mandela and Shimon Peres.

He is extraordinarily hands-on with the Forum's Board. I can hardly remember a meeting in which he did not participate – he is President of our International Business Council. Our Forum includes one hundred highly influential and respected business leaders, and he is its leader. That's something not so well known to the public.

Peter Brabeck is what is commonly referred to as a 'corporate statesman.' That means someone who, like a statesman, pays attention not only to his or her own affairs, but also gets involved in the context in which these affairs occur.

This includes, for example, his commitment to the question of water. He wanted to make this the focus of our January 2008 Davos meeting. Together we wrote an article about it. He is deeply convinced that water is more urgent than other environmental issues, because the impact of a water shortage can be quicker and more direct.

I find his commitment important. It is an expression of corporate citizenship. Nestlé gives expression to the fact that multinational companies are stakeholders in a global society. They have a duty to participate in finding solutions for the world's biggest problems. We do not have a world government, and therefore it is all the more important that governments and the large multinational corporations work together.

Peter Brabeck concentrates on the areas where he can contribute the most, both from his own and from Nestlé's perspective. So his commitment to the water question is not, as often portrayed in the media, because Nestlé has a vested interest in water, but because his work allows him to see what problems are approaching us. He acts from a genuine commitment as a Global Corporate Statesman.

How would you describe his business leadership style and his concept of leadership?

He is ready and able for radical change. But radical change must always be constructive, which means it must build on existing strengths not detract from them. That's how I would describe his general business philosophy.

It's not about creative destruction in Joseph Schumpeter's sense, who saw capitalism as creative destruction. It's more about the question: how can I change things faster by playing from strength? As I mentioned, Peter Brabeck's leadership style is shaped by clear vision, clear strategies and clear concepts for their implementation. These qualities win him the trust of other people and he does not need institutional support. He is perceived as a strong personality. Of course, his stature and presence are very important too.

I have led many discussion groups in which he was included. As chairman I always enjoy watching the participants. I noticed that Peter Brabeck is always very attentive to what is being said. He is very committed and alert. Unlike other people, he never glances at his cell phone during a meeting. He is always completely attentive, and naturally others are affected by the force of his personality.

A theme that strongly connects us is that of Global Corporate Citizenship. Peter Brabeck and I have often talked about the topic and we essentially have the same outlook. On one point we are opposed: he says that while we have an obligation to stakeholders, our first obligation is to long-term shareholder value, with emphasis on long-term.

I on the contrary believe that a business leader is not there primarily for the shareholders, but for all stakeholders. Although the latter all have different, sometimes short-term interests, they are unified by a common long-term interest, namely the long-term strengthening of the enterprise. But this is also in the shareholder's interest. With the recent launching of Nestlé's Creating Shared Value program, Brabeck has come much closer to this more comprehensive way of looking at a company's role. Employees and their families, suppliers, customers and consumers, especially in the communities where Nestlé is active, are all part of this shared value.

Perhaps our differences are somewhat theoretical; we have different starting points but come to the same conclusions. That conclusion is the long-term creation of value. For Peter Brabeck it is in the long-term interest of his firm to acknowledge its social responsibility; it's not just a PR campaign.

For me, a company has just as much of a duty to serve the stakeholders as the shareholders, and in the process, the interests of the latter are also protected.

What has shaped Mr. Brabeck's image most strongly in the public eye?
Certainly his striking appearance, but also his successes with Nestlé, which is recognized as a very successful enterprise. In addition, the fact that he is always shaping opinions, such as on the water issue. It's more than mere political correctness. When Brabeck speaks, you know it's coming from the heart. He's not aiming to please anyone or any political party. It's genuinely him.

What distinguishes Peter Brabeck the person?
I have three key words here: fact-oriented, solution-oriented and without blinders.

Does Mr. Brabeck follow a specific set of principles?
Loyalty. Ethics. Sincerity. He can quickly see through someone. If anyone wants to play games with him he will react negatively – that's the 'unpleasant transparency.' Results are more important to him than playing by the rules.

What do you value most in him?
Loyalty, directness, and instead of "unpleasant transparency," I prefer to use another term here which means the same thing: constructive criticism. What is the most astonishing thing about him? It's the combination of his background – coming from the mountain region of Kärnten (Carinthia), from a pure, natural world, and then a career which lifted him to the highest summits of the economy, a cosmopolitan career which raised him from the local to the global.

Today we say "be global, keep your local roots." That applies both to Brabeck the man and to the Nestlé firm. That's no coincidence, Nestlé is a firm which has always protected and nurtured its local roots and origins, and yet has also succeeded in becoming a global organization.

There are many parallels here with Mr. Brabeck, who has grown from his origins in Carinthia to take on a globally important role, not only economically but also in social policies which transcends his business role. I think that's the best way to summarize it. ”

How does one become the head of Nestlé?

The art of finding a successor

In the mid-1990s, the greatest worry facing Helmut Maucher was finding the right successor. Looking back on this in 2000 he commented, "Today I am delighted that I was successful, because Brabeck and his team are doing a good job. It is a well known fact that many people of strong character are not able to find a suitable successor; the biggest mistake they make is at the end of their career, by finding a weak replacement or none at all. There are countless such negative examples."

In a conversation with Egon Zehnder International management consultants in 1999, Helmut Maucher said, "A friendly team spirit is an important part of working together. It results in greater strength. Even if, as the leader, you must always keep a kind of distance, in case emotional problems arise when decisions are made that are in the interest of the firm. This happens to all of us sometime in our lives, and it is one of the most difficult chapters for someone who is as compassionate as I am."

In 1994, Helmut Maucher and Peter Brabeck had a conversation in which they spoke quite openly to each other, they both remember to this day.

Peter Brabeck recalls: "I was very happy out in the field. I was not particularly excited when Helmut Maucher brought me back to work in headquarters in 1987. However, I'm a good soldier and know that you have to go through certain stages, but I had always hoped to get back into the field; there were still a few large markets around the world that interested me as a challenge.

"So I went to him and told him that I had done my time here and wanted to get back out to the front line again. While we were on the subject he asked me quite directly, 'What is it that you want?' Without thinking, I replied, 'Since you asked, some day I want to sit where you are sitting.'"

Helmut Maucher notes: "Then I said, 'Okay, you are in the pipeline.' That was the job interview."

From then on, Helmut Maucher and Peter Brabeck had many confidential and intense conversations. After Peter Brabeck had become Director of Strategic Business Group 2 with responsibility for marketing and communication, he and Maucher jointly drew up the product strategy which is still in force today, including branding and communications policies.

Helmut Maucher: "At that time I saw him as my guiding intellectual force. He named the products we needed, the appropriate marketing strategy and where our communications were leading us." Peter Brabeck remembers Helmut Maucher jokingly giving him the title of "Suslov" after the old supreme ideologist of the Soviet communists.

When Peter Brabeck was brought to the group headquarters in Vevey, he had assumed that he would remain there for three years before taking over a bigger market. The fact that other prospects then opened up demanded a great deal of patience, self-discipline and a sense of duty. When he finally did succeed Helmut Maucher, it came as a surprise to many people because he had been Market Head of the small country of Venezuela and not of one of the big markets such as the USA or Germany.

Brabeck comments that markets in small countries should not be underestimated, because he had full responsibility there, something which would not necessarily have been the case for a division head in a larger country. At that time, Nestlé did not yet have a regional structure; the Market Head was directly responsible for everything that happened locally.

At the end of 1995, the change of CEO was officially announced and eighteen months remained for both men to discuss and agree on a strategy for future collaboration. The fact that Helmut Maucher dealt with the transition in such an excellent way throughout played a fundamental role. He discussed every major decision with Peter Brabeck, whether on personnel or strategy.

"That did require a degree of self-control on both sides," said Brabeck. "He brought me in and I accepted that until he definitively handed over the reins he was still the boss."

However, even after Brabeck became CEO in 1997, Helmut Maucher retained the role of so-called active chairman as Chairman of the Board of Directors until the year 2000 and continued to be fully involved in the executive concerns of the firm.

In 1999 Maucher commented, "We both agreed on which subjects he no longer needed to consult me and on which ones I still wanted to be consulted. That's transparent to everyone. (...)

"When you have headed up a company with all your heart and soul for as long as I have, it is emotionally difficult to just say one day, 'now someone else can do it.' After the changeover, I deliberately made myself scarce; I no longer haunted the corridors, thus people saw that I had distanced myself from the business. Eventually, over the final few years, I was able to prepare myself for the moment that I knew was coming.

"Perhaps in the end, that helped me to cope better than I had feared. Taking that step is certainly not easy for anyone. I stayed at the top longer than most people and yet stopping did not blow me away; I was not depressed, but I accepted it. Here in the office people even said 'we know Maucher, he'll never be able to quit.' They got quite a surprise."

In Helmut Maucher's opinion, as the boss you must be careful to prepare your successor and then keep to the agreed rules of the game, and not spoil the game for your successor. Many people think that the worst position to have is that of designated successor.

Peter Brabeck's comment was: "It must not be drawn out too long. For us, it took almost four years, without counting the unofficial part; I consider it best to go public eighteen months before the shareholders meeting."

But what skills do you actually need to successfully lead an enterprise as large as Nestlé? Peter Brabeck: "If you don't have a clear vision of the future, and if you can't turn ideas into strategies, or action; if you can't explain your goals and methods to others; if you don't have any natural authority and can't win your colleagues over to voluntary cooperation; if you can't comprehend the numbers, and finally if you do not sufficiently grasp the production process, you are not suited for the job."

Brabeck's career shows how he succeeded in meeting the standards he set for himself.

A solid foundation – 17 years' experience in Latin America

Peter Brabeck describes his 17 plus years in Latin America as extraordinarily important, for him personally and for his professional development. Without the experience gained there, he would never have been able to run Nestlé. Yet his professional career began in an unspectacular manner.

After completing his general education, he attended the Vienna University of Economics and Business and graduated with a Diploma in Business Administration. He was already interested in working abroad, so from the outset he looked for an employer who, unlike many of the nationalized firms in Austria, rated ability and achievement rather than political affiliation, as key factors.

He started in 1968 as a salesman of ice cream with Findus Jopa, a company that belonged to Nestlé at the time but had not been incorporated into the Group. Every morning he would load up his van and set off to visit his customers. He liked the work. He was his own boss all day and depended on his own skills for sales.

Later, when Findus Jopa was sold to Unilever, Peter Brabeck had the choice of staying with his former employer or moving to Nestlé.

He chose the latter option and applied for the job of National Sales Manager for the ice cream division in Chile.

For most Europeans, this position would not exactly be described as a dream job or even the foundation for a solid career.

There were few direct links between this country on the other side of the world and the Nestlé headquarters in Vevey. There was no internet or email communication, even the fax had not yet been invented. Letters took four to five weeks to arrive and sometimes it took months for an answer to be prepared. The quickest means of communication for urgent matters were the telex and the telephone; however, intercontinental conversations could only be conducted with the authorization of the Managing Director. Making a name for yourself inside the Company, but outside its national borders, was at that time virtually impossible for an individual employee.

As far as international enterprises were concerned the emerging political circumstances in Chile presented an even greater deterrent. In 1969, the Communists and Socialists, as well as a few small humanist-, left-Christian- and Marxist parties, formed an electoral alliance called the Unidad Popular. The UP followed a socialist line and campaigned for the nationalization of industry and the expropriation of big landowners. The future of foreign firms was uncertain. The same year that the Unidad Popular candidate, Salvador Allende, was elected President, Peter Brabeck took up his position as ice cream salesman in Chile.

Brabeck describes the situation in Chile at that time: "Allende was leading a coalition government with 37 percent of the vote, split into seven parties which shared little common ground politically. There was, in fact, no common political power base. Each party did what it wanted, each party had one or two ministries and the ministries likewise did what they wanted." Brabeck knew Allende very well and he sometimes went directly to him with his requests; Allende would then tell him which minister he should speak to.

There was a complete vacuum, leading the country to bankruptcy within two years. There was nothing to buy in the legitimate markets. You had to stand in line for 48 hours for a few liters of oil, the supermarkets were empty, everything was done by barter. The country was totally paralyzed by a general strike. If a firm stopped production and no longer looked after the land, it was in danger of simply being nationalized.

Therefore it was very important for a firm to continue operating. As long as it was producing, it would not be nationalized. However, without raw materials this was impossible and raw materials were allocated by a ministry which would set prices in dollars. Moreover, different ministries were responsible for different materials, and were controlled by different political parties.

Brabeck spent over 80 percent of his time running from one ministry to another to guarantee supplies of raw materials, obtain dollars for the purchases and checking into prices. The unions in Chile were also very strong at the time, and groups calling themselves Friends of Unidad Popular were organized within every firm, repeatedly calling for strike actions when something did not meet their demands.

In the residential quarters, there were Junta de Vecinos, so-called neighborhood associations which functioned like the block wardens of the former East Germany. When there was nothing left to eat, they would distribute baskets of food to the residents of the neighborhoods. Anyone wanting a basket had to register and was thus subjected to stringent controls.

Brabeck says that leading the Company through this period was not easy but was interesting. At that time within Nestlé the traditional Nestlé business was still separate from the ice cream and frozen food businesses. In Chile, these were Nestlé Chile and the ice cream firm Savory, for which Brabeck worked during his first years.

It was a small business with no division between the head office and the factory. Production, distribution, sales and the development laboratory were all in the same factory. Brabeck worked side by side with all the employees every day. The salesmen loaded the goods directly from the factory onto the trucks, often in the middle of the night.

It was quite an adventure, Brabeck remembers, but the best thing was being able to develop new initiatives. He had free rein and could innovate and experiment in many ways, not only on the product side but also in marketing, advertising and distribution. He was constantly on the move in a country that stretches over 4,300 kilometers from north to south – equivalent to the distance from the North Pole to the Sahara.

Peter Brabeck was the first to open a land route to Tierra del Fuego. Along the way, trucks had to cross a strip of Argentine territory. The journey took six days on dirt roads. To prevent the ice cream in the trucks from melting, they had to organize stopovers with electricity for charging the refrigeration units.

The fact that he was working at the grassroots and therefore knew exactly what the problems were, is important for Brabeck. The marketing people were not just spinning theories, he says. And if the laboratory, production, sales, marketing, and advertising managers are all in the same location with the salespeople, they quickly learn that to work well they must work as a team. One important experience for Brabeck was that right from the start, he was able to collaborate on ideas and decisions with the team and include everyone's assessments. He is convinced that this integrated view of the work is what made the whole firm so successful. It's growth rate was very high, and its profitability among the highest. Even today, Savory has a higher market value than Coca-Cola in Chile. Wherever you go, from Tierra del Fuego right to the edge of the desert, you see Savory ice cream everywhere. It is the most famous brand in Chile.

Chile has the highest consumption of ice cream per capita in Latin America and the tenth highest worldwide. On average, each Chilean consumes six liters of ice cream a year. That may also be because its cost is only one quarter of the world average.

"Ice cream is exceptionally strong in Chile because, during that period, we claimed every sales territory that already existed, and some that did not yet exist," says Brabeck. Ice freezers were put everywhere: in schools, at swimming pools and in kiosks.

"We developed a culture similar to what we had had in Europe in the past. Unlike the competition, we made our products available everywhere, rather than just relying on sales through supermarkets." Otherwise, Brabeck is convinced, "we would have lost our powerful market presence. A consumer will go no further than 200 meters to buy an ice cream, therefore the industry has to be organized accordingly. We worked through the whole country, from Santiago through the beaches at Valparaiso, down to Tierra del Fuego."

It was during that time that the Nestlé principle "whenever, wherever, however" was created. Sales of instant noodles or Maggi cubes continue today throughout the world based on the same principle. "Whether you are in Burkina Faso or in Sierra Leone," says Peter Brabeck, "you will come across Nestlé products everywhere. In retrospect, Peter Brabeck reflects, we were really ahead of our times even by European standards." There was a great deal of freedom. One product launched for the Savory business was what Brabeck called "Kukulina ice cream." To promote Kukulina, a live, 2-hour TV show was produced which ran for eighteen weeks. Like the product, the show was called Kukulina, where musicians from around the country could compete in the South American version of the Eurovision Song Contest. The television audience would choose the winner who would then officially represent Chile.

"This television project used up the entire year's marketing budget. I don't know if that would make anyone very happy today. At the time, it was a genuine marketing innovation which even today," Brabeck is convinced, "could not be done in Europe." But what was so exciting for him was having the freedom to do such things and to improvise, however he also had to risk the consequences. You can still see segments of the Kukulina show from 1975 today on YouTube.

Peter Brabeck was also very active in Chilean organizations, for example as Chairman of the Marketing Association and the Advertising Association. He experienced Allende's term of office (1970–1973) and then, after Allende's overthrow, that of Augusto Pinochet. In 1975, Brabeck was transferred to the Nestlé headquarters in Vevey but only three months later he returned. The job of Marketing Director needed to be filled, but since no one wanted to go to Pinochet's Chile, Brabeck went back. It was a big opportunity for him to rise from ice cream sales to Marketing Director of Nestlé Chile.

Latin America left its mark on him – Conversation with Ernesto Zedillo

Ernesto Zedillo Ponce de Léon, born 1951, studied economics at the Polytechnic in Mexico City and at Yale University, where he earned a doctorate. In 1978, he joined the Mexican Central Bank and, in 1987, became Secretary in the Planning Ministry. In 1988, he was appointed Planning Minister and, in 1992, Minister of Education. From 1988, Zedillo was involved with the national development plan for economic, financial and social recovery and set up the prerequisites for Mexico's admittance to the North American free trade zone, NAFTA. From 1994 to the end of 2000, he was President of Mexico. He subsequently worked as consultant for various international businesses and organizations. Today, Dr. Zedillo is Director of the Center for the Study of Globalization at Yale University and is one of the leading voices on the subject of globalization, and among other things, member of the Foundation Board of the World Economic Forum.

“ ***Do you remember the first time you met Peter Brabeck?***
It was early on when I was President of Mexico. Peter was introduced to me by Helmut Maucher and Carlos Eduardo Represas during a visit to Mexico.

Are there any joint activities or joint projects with Peter Brabeck at the World Economic Forum that you remember particularly fondly?
What I remember most about Peter was his enthusiasm about undertaking new projects in Mexico at a time when things were

not going particularly well in the Mexican economy. Peter trusted the Mexican people and its government and he was right. The projects he launched were proven right, including one in a state, Chiapas, that was affected by serious conflict at the time.

You're familiar with Peter Brabeck and Nestlé's Creating Shared Value projects in Latin America. Do you see any effects on the social and economic situation of the people living there?
I know of it and it's a great example of Peter's leadership in the field of social responsibility. I like to think that somehow Nestlé's work in Mexico was a source of inspiration for that initiative.

How would you describe the current political and economic situation in Latin America?
With a few regrettable exceptions, Latin America has emerged from the recent economic crisis with a new sense of confidence. The reforms undertaken some years ago gave to our region a resilience that allowed us to withstand the worst global crisis since the end of World War II. As a whole, Latin America will retake the path of reasonable, although not spectacular, growth this year. If the process of reform is revived, then the region will become a significant driver of global growth within the next few years.

How do you see the role of Nestlé and Peter Brabeck in the global economy and society?
Nestlé is a great consumer products company, and I say this with the authority accorded to me by being part, as an independent board director, of another outstanding consumer oriented company, P&G. Obviously, Peter is now part of Nestlé's remarkable history and contribution to people's wellbeing.

Do you see a change in the role of global enterprises in the future?
What I see is more competition globally and this will make companies not only deliver better products to their customers and good results to their shareholders, but also strive to be good global citizens.

Can you tell me something about Peter Brabeck as a person?
Peter is certainly a remarkable business leader, but, more importantly – at least for me – he is a good human being worried about the most serious problems of our world and willing to do something to address them. As a friend, I enjoy his love of music, sports and his somehow "Latin Americanized" sense of humor.

Is there something which, in your opinion, must absolutely be included in this book?
I wish that you would emphasize that Peter is an Austrian, very proud of his country, living and working in Switzerland and traveling with ease all over the world. He is really a fine Austrian global citizen. ”

How to turn an export company into a consumer goods company

From 1981 to 1983, Peter Brabeck was CEO of Nestlé Ecuador. There were two particular challenges there, he reports. At the time, Nestlé Ecuador was a joint venture with a local group which held 49 percent of the share capital. Nestlé also held 49 percent and the remaining 2 percent was distributed among investors. The Chairman of the Board of Directors was a representative of the local partner.

Peter Brabeck first had to learn that as CEO he had to reflect not only the interests of Nestlé but also acknowledge those of the local partner, and reach a consensus. He recognized that a business in such a host country would be successful if it created value not only for its own shareholders but also for local interests. This sounds relatively simple but is actually not so easy, says Brabeck.

As an example, he cites the cost of an expatriate employee who wished to spend his holiday with his family in his home country and who therefore wanted to receive part of his salary in a stable currency. In a country with an inflation rate of 60 percent this meant lengthy discussions in the Board of Directors. It was hard for local shareholders to accept that a few foreign employees cost more than the far bigger factory work force. "You simply have to learn to act diplomatically with the different groups and find a balance," says Brabeck. For him it was an important learning period, balancing between the strong local interests and those of the multinational parent company. Regional considerations, not just in marketing but also social demands, were later enshrined in the Creating Shared Value concept. "These are experiences that you take with you," says Brabeck. "In the long run, you can't be successful for your shareholders if you don't continually strive to create value for the community."

The second challenge for Brabeck in Ecuador lay in completely reorganizing the business from an export orientation to domestic sales. Initially, over 80 percent of Nestlé Ecuador's output was for export. The factory made mainly chocolate from cocoa – not the finished product but semi-finished (cocoa powder) – and sold it abroad. As a result, it was heavily dependent on the local price for cocoa and on the price at which cocoa could be sold on the international market. Hedging on the futures market was therefore very important. When Peter Brabeck was offered the job of heading up the company, it had just suffered a huge hedging loss and was actually bankrupt.

He first had to learn how the international raw materials market functions. In a second phase, he convinced the shareholders to give up the export business and concentrate on domestic sales of consumer goods in Ecuador. "It was an important strategic decision for us at the time," Brabeck stresses.

The local partner then took over the international business and concentrated fully on processing raw material into semi-finished products, while Brabeck slowly transformed the cocoa factory from semi-finished products to finished products for the domestic consumption market. Managing this change was probably his most important experience in Ecuador, he says. He also learned a lot about raw materials and their markets which greatly helped him later as CEO in Vevey, because this is extremely important for senior management. "The fact that we have years of experience in these raw materials markets is probably also the reason why we understand them a little better than some of our competitors," says Brabeck.

Nestlé Ecuador thus shed its export burden and could hand over the whole international business to its local partner which is still a Nestlé supplier to this day.

Ecuador consists of two very different geographical regions – the coastal area where trading was done traditionally and where industry has become established; and the highlands where the Indians live. The coastal area has tropical temperatures, its main products are raw sugar and rum, while slightly higher up you find coffee and cocoa. Arriba cocoa is one of the best in the world. On the high plateau, corn and wheat are grown, and at the very top, potatoes.

Nestlé had a cocoa factory on the coast and a milk factory in the highlands producing mainly fresh milk and cheese and, later, dried milk. To guarantee the supply of raw materials, Nestlé worked with the farmers, setting up milk districts. This pioneering project was also approved of by the government because it brought a fixed income to the farmers in these very remote parts of the country. The biggest problem at the time was negotiating with the Indian unions. They were Otavalenos, the only highland Indians who had not been conquered by the Incas and to this day, as a visible sign of their invincibility, they still wear their hair long. When the Incas conquered a race they allowed the conquered considerable freedom, but cut off their hair as a sign that they were their subjects.

Brabeck had to negotiate with the Otavalenos. "They know how to negotiate," says Brabeck. "They sit around the table all day long and just look down; they never look at you so you have no idea what they are thinking." It was not easy to gain their confidence, win them over and lead them in the right direction. "I learned endless patience from it," says Brabeck. With this patience and a great deal of work, the milk district was set up. Today about 2,500 farmers make their living there, and thanks to technical help and advice, produce 265 kilograms of milk per day per farmer. Fifteen years ago, the daily amount of milk produced per farmer was only 61 kilograms.

How a new company emerged from a nationalized one

From 1983 to 1987, Peter Brabeck was Chairman and Chief Executive Officer of Espalsa, later reorganized into Nestlé Venezuela. When he took over the post in 1983, Nestlé was still in negotiations with the government concerning the mid-1970s nationalization of its then large subsidiary, Indulac, which had reduced Nestlé's presence in Venezuela to the comparatively small Espalsa company. Compensation for this was still outstanding. While Indulac was the leading milk business in the country and had pioneered the setting up of milk districts since 1944, Espalsa produced and sold cereals, Maggi and Nescafé. As CEO of Espalsa, Brabeck's task was to further develop Nestlé's activities, and as Chairman, he was also supposed to bring the nationalization negotiations to a positive and constructive conclusion, to open the door for broader Nestlé activity.

During his time in South America, Peter Brabeck learned that it was extremely important to stay in contact with institutions and be well-connected with governments. In these countries, the survival and success of a business depended very heavily on government decisions. Supplies of raw materials, pricing, and even marketing were under state control.

In Venezuela, among other positions, Brabeck was a member of the Venezuelan Chamber of Commerce Supervisory Board, Chairman of the Chamber in charge of foreign investment, and Vice-President of the Latin American Chamber of Commerce. He was also Member, Director and Vice-President of the Inter-American Trade Association, which was the chamber for industry for all of North and South America.

He represented Venezuela at the highest level on many committees and thus had good access to the government. Often he also represented private industry and, in doing so, again worked closely with the government. "It helps, for example, if you can speak personally with a minister who sets prices," says Brabeck, and you learn to develop diplomatic skills. This also changed his conception of the role of private industry in society.

In Latin America, Brabeck learned to handle both unions and politicians. In Chile, the challenge was to develop a business during politically difficult times. Later, in Ecuador, he had to transform a firm which only produced for export into a domestic consumer goods firm. In Venezuela, the Nestlé milk business was nationalized; Brabeck had to see these negotiations to their conclusion, and establish the new Nestlé Venezuela. He thinks these experiences contributed much to developing his personal world view and leadership abilities.

In 1987, Peter Brabeck returned to the Nestlé headquarters in Vevey and took over the management of the culinary products division. In 1992, he was appointed General Manager responsible for the newly created strategic business group, comprising food (culinary products), chocolate, confectionery and ice cream, pet food and the Buitoni brand.

"When all was said and done, we always found ourselves on common ground" – Conversation with Rainer E. Gut

Rainer E. Gut, born 1932, gained his first professional experience with Crédit Commercial de France in Paris, the First National City Bank in London and the Schweizerische Bankgesellschaft (SBG) in Zurich.

In 1968, he became a general partner of Lazard Frères & Co. in New York and in 1971, Chairman and CEO of the Swiss American Corporation in New York, a former holding company of Credit Suisse, involved in investment banking in the USA.

In 1973, he was called to Credit Suisse's headquarters in Zurich and appointed member of the Board. In 1977 he was appointed Speaker of the Executive Board and was elected as its President in 1982. From 1983 to 2000, he was the Chairman of the Board of Directors of Credit Suisse, Zurich; from 1988 to 2000, he was also Chairman of the Board of Directors of Credit Suisse First Boston; and, from 1988 to 2000, Chairman of the Board of Directors of Credit Suisse Group AG (formerly CS Holding), whose Honorary Chairman he has been since 2000.

Rainer E. Gut was a member of Nestlé S.A.'s Board of Directors from 1981 to 2005. In 1988, he was elected to the inner circle, the Chairman's Committee, and in 1991 became 1st Vice-Chairman of the Board. From 2000 to 2005, he led the enterprise as Chairman of the Board of Directors.

“ ***How familiar were you with Nestlé, and with Brabeck, when you became Chairman of the Board?***

I'll have to go back some years here. When I was called to the Nestlé Board in 1981, Helmut Maucher was taking over the role of Board Delegate, and later Chairman of the Board. I myself was elected to the Chairman's Committee in 1988 and became its Vice Chairman in 1991.

These were probably Nestlé's most defining twenty years of the last century. The Company was newly positioned and operating very close to the market so that it was able to become the biggest food company in the world. I was very familiar with Nestlé by the year 2000 when I was to assume the Chairmanship for five years.

During those years I closely followed Peter Brabeck's career until he became Chairman of the Board. A relationship of trust emerged between us over the years, which also applied to many other members of management. There were no reservations in this. Nestlé always comes first – at all levels of the Company in every country – and a small-minded approach is absolutely out of place.

The years passed, and Peter Brabeck led the Company as CEO with great success and "ease" – this should be understood as a great compliment, for Brabeck is a remarkable and striking multi-faceted personality.

What do you mean by that?

He's solidly grounded; he knows his roots, his goals. Peter works hard; he lives intensely (mountain climbing, for example) and has found a harmonious balance between his personal and professional life.

His natural intelligence and seemingly inexhaustible genuine interest in the economy, world politics, art and culture, philosophy, his erudition, and much more, have contributed to his well-grounded knowledge in many important areas. That's why Peter is highly valued as a strong discussion partner even outside the Company, for example at the World Economic Forum in Davos, the European Round Table, the WTO, the UN and so on. What sets him apart is his optimism and his genuine interest in people and nature.

What is less well known is that Peter values the exchange of ideas with a simple ice cream salesman or with a shepherd on a remote mountainside as much as with an orchestra conductor, a CEO or a government representative. He addresses mankind's problems and is committed to development aid as well as the protection of nature and the climate. Nestlé earns money with natural resources, for example water. Peter campaigns, with measurable results, to ensure that water is accessible even to the poorest of the poor.

Brabeck has had a remarkable career within the Company – did he deliberately force his way up?

Absolutely not. He always put the Company's interests first and took his role very seriously. I'd like to give an example here: when the topic of who would succeed Helmut Maucher as Chairman of the Board came up, and I was officially asked by Helmut to take over the chairmanship, I initially had some doubts as to whether I should accept or not. I didn't want to step on Peter's toes, and so I said I would like to have a one-to-one discussion with him.

He convinced me to take the job, for at the time he was concentrating on defining the future of Nestlé's operations as CEO, implementing company strategy; he also wanted to have some key positions occupied during this new phase. Brabeck's spontaneous and sincere approval of my selection as Chairman was what ultimately moved me to take the job. I never regretted it – on the contrary, my close collaboration with Peter Brabeck under Nestlé's roof was a happy conclusion to my professional career.

I imagine that collaboration between two such strong personalities is not simple?

The word 'simple' hides the complexity of our collaboration. I can try to describe it: it's enjoyable to work with Peter on a daily basis. He's efficient, full of determination, communicative and a born fighter. And despite enormous pressures he's almost always in a good mood and open to ideas and constructive criticism. He is an outstanding sparring partner in the decision-making process. Not that he's easily convinced, but rather a very strong "negotiating partner"/CEO!

He is able to go over impending decisions again and again, until he is absolutely certain: "Yes, that's the right decision." That doesn't mean he hesitates, but that he makes his decisions after sound research, thought through in detail, having explored all the possible consequences.

In all the years that I was Chairman of the Board and Peter was CEO, not a single matter was put to the Board on which we had not reached a consensus. For every acquisition, every change in strategy, every personnel decision and so on, we were in absolute agreement. This agreement, at a time when decisions – particularly in the area of mergers and acquisitions – always had to be made in the shortest of time spans due to the rapidly changing market, presupposes an unlimited mutual trust and also the willingness to openly present each other with the pros and cons.

What still connects you to Peter Brabeck today?
We have a friendship which is based on complete trust. I value our regular meetings in Vevey a great deal. I am extremely grateful for his committed and skillful guidance of Nestlé into a successful future. ”

CEO and Chairman of the Board – fighting for the double mandate

In 1998 the decision had been made that the banker, Rainer E. Gut, who had been a member of the Nestlé Board of Directors since 1981, would take the position as non-executive Chairman in the year 2000 and stay in that position until 2005. Peter Brabeck was the key figure in this decision, going back to a discussion with Egon Zehnder International GmbH consultants in 1999, in which Helmut Maucher said: "If Rainer Gut had not been Brabeck's first choice, we would not have appointed him and in any case he would not have accepted the position."

During that discussion, Peter Brabeck said that he considered four points in making his choice: "First, that an enterprise like ours needs a Chairman who really knows the company. Second, he should be available to serve for a reasonable period, because changing Chairmen every two years is quite taxing on the CEO. Third, the Board of Directors should be led by someone who offers the company additional competence and experience. Rainer E. Gut is worldly-wise, has been through very difficult situations, did a lot for Switzerland and with his commanding authority, will be a terrific Nestlé representative. Finally, the fourth and most important point for me is interpersonal chemistry and particularly in this respect he was my ideal candidate."

Maucher then added: "When Rainer E. Gut retires, Peter will be 60. Then he can decide whether to present himself as a candidate for the chairmanship. We have therefore deliberately left open whether the posts of Chairman and CEO should be separate or held by one person. It's a case by case question. I have done it all; first I was CEO, then both, and now only Chairman.

"The belief that combining the two positions means that one person will have unlimited power, is utter nonsense. For like it or not, the person at the top will be controlled by his own employees and his colleagues on the Board. No one can fight against the entire team; a consensus must somehow be achieved."

"Moreover, the Chairman's Committee, which always consists of independent people, has the formal right and authority to set limits on absolute power and act accordingly. If I had gone mad, they would have been able to go over my head and do the right thing. This control must always be there in some form or other."

When, as planned, Rainer E. Gut retired from the chairmanship in 2005 for reasons of age, the Board of Directors decided that Peter Brabeck, who was already Vice Chairman of the Board of Directors as well as CEO, should take over the position, which also required the approval of the shareholders' meeting.

Helmut Maucher himself had held the double mandate from 1990 to 1997. Now, however, it suddenly provoked vehement public criticism. The spokesman for the opponents was Dominique Biedermann who, with his Swiss investors foundation, Ethos, represented Swiss pension funds, holding about 875 million Swiss francs worth of shares. He was against concentrating power in the hands of one man and demanded that the CEO should answer not only to the Board of Directors but to the Chairman as well.

Peter Brabeck then threatened to resign as CEO if the motion against the double mandate was carried by the shareholders' meeting and the separation of the two positions was forced through. The entire Nestlé Board of Directors would then resign as well. In the end, in round figures, 50 percent of the shareholders present voted for the double mandate, 14 percent abstained and 36 percent voted against.

In his professional life, Peter Brabeck had only one complete disagreement with what the press wrote about him, and that was during the campaign against the double mandate. In his opinion, the facts were deliberately misrepresented. The headline read: "Brabeck wants a double mandate so that he can earn 30 million francs." This set the public against him and people virtually spat on him in the street and sent him threatening letters.

There was political intrigue going on behind his back among the shareholders. The relevant interested parties wanted to change the Corporate Governance system in Switzerland which would result in weakening the Board of Directors and strengthening the power of the shareholders. Brabeck believes that this campaign is still ongoing,, only with new actors in the limelight. In the final analysis however, Nestlé's successes under the double mandate proved it was the right decision.

"Nestlé has a very strong Board of Directors," Brabeck emphasizes. "Our fourteen board members are all leading figures in business and society and have a wide range of expertise. Any opinion that they are irrelevant is wide off the mark."

He fully agrees that, in principle, separating the posts of Chairman of the Board and CEO is a good solution, provided that four criteria are met:

First, the Chairman must understand the business. Brabeck thinks it is completely mistaken to believe, as the British for example do, that the Chairman of the Board does not need to understand the business. Having someone from a consumer goods industry be put into the auto industry, and from the auto industry into pharmaceuticals is counterproductive.

Second, is that the Chairman should stay in his position for a certain length of time. Brabeck is absolutely opposed to bringing in a new Chairman every year, since he could not fulfill the main responsibility of a Board member, i.e. to guide the company's long-term strategy. Board members must be in their position for at least four or five years to achieve anything at all.

Third, the Chairman of the Board must be a personality who can represent the company to the outside world. That in Brabeck's view, is important and becoming more so. Because his task is to represent the shareholders, he must be capable of not merely staying in contact with major shareholders but also with government offices.

Fourth and perhaps the most important point for Peter Brabeck, is the personal chemistry between the CEO and the Chairman. If this is not good, there will be too many frictional losses.

If these four requirements are met, then Brabeck thinks separating the positions of Chairman and CEO is a good thing. Otherwise it is not.

At the time, the double mandate was the right solution because of the particular combination of circumstances, Brabeck explains, saying that in 2005 Nestlé was in the middle phase of major strategic change – the transformation from food and beverages into a nutrition, health and wellness business. As CEO he had initiated this transformation and the Board wanted him to see it through to the end.

Brabeck is convinced that if a new CEO had been appointed, he would have lacked freedom of action. And conversely, a new Chairman heading the Board merely for the sake of Corporate Governance, could have exercised virtually no influence on this strategic process. This was the reason for deciding on a double mandate as a three to four year interim solution.

Helmut Maucher: "I chose the best person as my successor"

Helmut Maucher was born in 1927. After finishing a business apprenticeship at a milk company in Eisenharz in Westallgäu, the company was bought up by Nestlé. He ultimately moved on to work at Nestlé in Frankfurt, where in addition to his job he studied business part-time and obtained a Master's Degree in Business Administration. From 1964 to 1980, he remained there holding a number of different positions, before finally becoming General Manager of the Nestlé group in Germany in 1975.

In 1980, Maucher moved to Nestlé headquarters in Vevey as General Manager and Member of the Executive Committee; one year later he became CEO. From 1990 to 1997, Maucher served as both Chairman and Chief Executive Officer. After retiring as CEO, he remained Chairman of the Board until 2000, when he was made Honorary Chairman. He holds honorary doctorates from the European Business School in Oestrich-Winkel, the Technical University in Munich and the Autonomous University in Guadalajara, Mexico.

Helmut Maucher is one of the few legendary European managers who continues to be remembered years after his retirement from active business life. He will always be "Mr. Nestlé," a man of experience and a marketing man, whose razor-sharp powers of judgment, integrity, charm and wit continue to win people's hearts.

He frankly acknowledges that it would have been difficult for anyone to follow him, but that Peter Brabeck was the best of the best. Maucher had noticed Brabeck when he was still a marketing manager in South America, and brought him to Vevey as head of the Strategic Business Unit for culinary products to give him the opportunity to gain international experience and to prove himself.

Maucher admits that he would have liked Peter Brabeck to have headed a large European market for a while, but as head of the culinary division and later of all Strategic Business Units, Brabeck had taken on so many different responsibilities that Helmut Maucher considered him to be well-qualified to become CEO.

Together Helmut Maucher and Peter Brabeck proceeded to fundamentally redesign Nestlé's existing brand and image, which still is reflected in the Company's success to this day. While Helmut Maucher was still CEO, Peter Brabeck was already promoting Nestlé's entry into the water business. He was ridiculed for this by many competitors because few recognized the opportunities it offered. As CEO, Helmut Maucher predicted three major resource shortages in the world: energy, water and cereals. The last two were essential components of Nestlé's business. Maucher had also brought into the portfolio or had established product groups with growth potential, such as ice cream, pet food and cereals, and strengthened Nestlé's weak presence in some countries by acquisitions, including the USA, and put Nestlé's name into partially blank areas on the map.

While public consciousness focused on energy problems early on, it is mainly due to Peter Brabeck that politicians and companies throughout the world have become increasingly aware of the water and agriculture problems. Helmut Maucher thinks Nestlé should take the lead in the field of personalized nutrition research. Proper nutrition is going to take on increasing importance especially for people in highly industrialized countries. Just what that individual diet will be, is still an open question, but it will play an increasingly important role in the prevention and treatment of certain diseases.

Since he retired from active business life, Helmut Maucher has refrained almost entirely from speaking publicly on operational matters, though he still keeps in touch with the Company's activities. He is happy that in the current period of crisis Peter Brabeck and Paul Bulcke are heading the Company and complementing each other so outstandingly.

He says that Peter Brabeck has the nerves to survive even difficult situations and to superbly cope with dangers. He has become the symbol of the Nestlé image, based on responsible conduct.

He adds that while Peter Brabeck emphasizes matters relating to the Board of Directors and supervising major strategies, Bulcke is more concerned with operations. As for the tasks and functions of the Board of Directors and Management, Maucher points out that, in addition to their normal functions, the Board should especially keep their eye on long-term implementation of strategic decisions and measures, since financial pressures and competition may make the decisions by the manager of operations somewhat short-sighted.

Nothing should be left to chance – planning the succession

The difference in the leadership styles of Helmut Maucher and Peter Brabeck manifested itself when finding a successor to Brabeck as CEO. Helmut Maucher had prepared the decisive template for his successor as CEO four years before the fact, and then organized a seamless transition, only relinquishing 80 percent of his authority in operational decision-making, since he still held the position of Chairman of the Board and defined his role as an active one.

Peter Brabeck went about it quite differently, as he explained in a conversation with Credit Suisse's "CS Bulletin" in early 2009. He stressed that the process of succession had been very important in Nestlé. There are two kinds of such successions. In the case of an emergency replacement, anyone can be replaced within 24 hours by a Deputy who can do an equivalent job at least in the short term.

This procedure is intended mainly for cases of illness but was also used when Mario Corti, the financial director, left to take over the role of CEO at Swissair from one day to the next, or when Paul Polman became CEO of Unilever.

In Nestlé, normal succession planning was amongst the most important strategic tasks. A system was developed to allow to track 2,400 employees. The Executive Board devotes two sessions a year exclusively to questions of succession and the Board of Directors devotes one session. Every Nestlé manager has the right to be heard and also the responsibility of being involved in naming his own successor. Nothing is left to chance.

The process of finding the right person to succeed Brabeck as CEO lasted about eighteen months. First, a list of potential internal and external candidates was drawn up. After the initial scrutiny, one external and five internal candidates remained. In the summer of 2007 the Nomination Committee, chaired by Board Member Peter Böckli, produced a shortlist of only two names – Paul Bulcke and Paul Polman – and in September the Board decided on Paul Bulcke.

Brabeck was not on the Nomination Committee, but naturally he knew all the candidates very well. He had met Paul Bulcke in Latin America twenty-five years before. He had met Paul Polman in the Groupe d'Ouchy in Lausanne where, since 1972, the top managers of the world's major brand companies have been meeting three times a year to exchange views, and Polman had impressed Brabeck with his strategic and innovative thinking. They also shared personal interests. For instance, after climbing Mount Kilimanjaro with blind and handicapped mountaineers, Polman had formed the Kilimanjaro Blind Trust, a foundation which supports blind children in East Africa.

Peter Brabeck insists that he always kept his personal opinions to himself, right up to the final decision. However, insiders are sure that he had his favorite.

The two final candidates were made of very different stuff. The Belgian Paul Bulcke came to Nestlé in 1979 as a marketing trainee; in 1980, he went to South America for sixteen years as director of Sales and Marketing in Chile, Ecuador and Peru. The similarities to Peter Brabeck are unmistakable. He then became Market Head in Portugal, the Czech Republic, Slovakia and Germany. In 2004, he moved to Vevey as Executive Vice President with responsibility for North and South America. Thus he steadily climbed the Nestlé success ladder. Like Peter Brabeck, Paul Bulcke has strong emotional ties to Nestlé and fully identifies with the organization. Paul Polman, who is two years younger than Bulcke, was with the American consumer goods company Procter & Gamble from 1986 to 2006, finishing as Group President for Europe. When Polman left Procter & Gamble, Brabeck invited him to join Nestlé, offering him the position of Chief Financial Officer, so that he could get to know the Company in all its complexity as quickly as possible. Polman accepted the offer, clearly in the hope of soon becoming CEO.

This expectation was not fulfilled. Polman took over Bulcke's position as head of the Zone Americas when the latter moved into the CEO's office. But in 2008 he went to Unilever as CEO. Naturally Paul Polman would have liked to have become CEO of Nestlé, says Brabeck. But in choosing his successor the defining question was not who was the better candidate but who the company needed in its current situation. "In our case, Paul Bulcke was the right man and in Unilever's case, Paul Polman," says Brabeck.

Polman's strength lies in crisis management and innovative renovation, Brabeck went on to say. He needs to be able to move things around. It was therefore no surprise to Brabeck that Unilever made him their CEO. The situation of that company was tailor-made for him. In contrast, Bulcke is a continuity manager. Brabeck is convinced that if Nestlé had been in a crisis and had to make radical cuts and changes, Polman would have been the right man. But as Nestlé was not in crisis but growing, Bulcke was the top choice. Peter Brabeck had carefully chosen a procedural style completely different from that of Helmut Maucher's to find a successor, but the succession itself was equally important to him: "I will have achieved nothing if my successor is not at least as successful as I was – and hopefully even more so. It's no great leadership achievement if a company runs well only when you are at the wheel."

Brabeck maintains that you should not expect your successor to be like you. Your successor must create a successful future, while your successes are now in the past and that is the difference. New challenges require a new leadership. Therefore the procedure for every succession should begin with defining the future profile of the company, as Nestlé did.

Clearly, the Nomination Committee believed that Paul Bulcke would fit the future profile of Nestlé better than Polman, and Peter Brabeck entirely agrees with this decision. He says that handing over the reins was not difficult for him and, as Chairman of the Board, he is not even Executive Chairman: "I really don't get involved in the day-to-day business." Instead the Board and Peter Brabeck have put new and challenging content into the position of Chairman.

Nestlé's Management and Leadership Principles

In June 1997, "The Nestlé Management and Leadership Principles" were published. This document was prepared and signed jointly by Maucher and Brabeck. It was no coincidence that the publication coincided with Peter Brabeck's becoming CEO. The document was to establish continuity and demonstrate that, with a change of management, the fundamental values of the enterprise continued to be valid. The requirements for a Nestlé manager as set out in the document are:

- courage, nerve, maintaining one's composure under pressure
- ability to learn, a feeling for innovation and empathy
- communication skills and skills in motivating and encouraging employees
- able to create an innovative climate
- thinking laterally
- credibility: in other words "practice what you preach"
- willingness to accept changes and capacity to steer a new course
- international experience and understanding of other cultures

- wide-ranging interests
- good general education
- responsible behavior and appearance, and good health.

The Nestlé culture is the subject of the comprehensive final chapter. It goes back to the founder of the Company, Henri Nestlé (1814–1890), who became intensely interested in local eating habits during his international business career, and developed an attitude of treating the traditions of other countries with respect. Right from the founding of the Company, there were already hints of the future Creating Shared Value concept: global thinking and global strategies but first and foremost, local business and local involvement.

The Swiss origins of the Nestlé culture are manifested in the following characteristics of its entrepreneurial leadership:

- pragmatic rather than dogmatic
- realistic initiatives and decisions based on facts, not fantasies or illusions
- relationships based on trust, mutual frankness and avoiding intrigue
- personal, direct mutual communication
- modesty, style and a sense of quality
- openness to future trends but also respect for basic human values
- skepticism towards short-term trends and self-styled "gurus".

Nestlé Basic Management and Leadership Principles (extracts, 1997)

General Principles

"Nestlé is not a faceless company marketing to faceless consumers. It is a human company providing a response to individual human needs the world over."

"Nestlé is more people- and product-oriented than systems-oriented. Systems are necessary and useful but should never be an end in themselves."

Shareholder Value
"Although Nestlé is committed to create value for its shareholders, it does not favor short-term profit and shareholder value maximization at the expense of long-term successful business development. Nestlé is however aware of the need to generate a reasonable profit each year."

Restructuring
"Nestlé is committed to the concept of continuous improvement of its activities, thus avoiding as much as possible emergency measures and abrupt changes."

Leadership
"We need a team with a leader and not a team as a leader (teamwork with responsible leadership) at every level of the organization."

Delegation
"Members of the Nestlé Management at all levels are more concerned with continuously adding value to the company than with exercising formal authority. They delegate what can be delegated without abdicating their responsibility."

Information
"Involvement of Nestlé's employees at all levels starts with appropriate information and communication about the overall activities of the company and the specific aspects of their work. Any changes and potential improvements should be discussed and ex-

plained. People should be invited to contribute their ideas to the process."

Criteria for Promotion
"Apart from professional skills and experience, the capacity and willingness to apply these principles are the main criteria for promotion, not a person's citizenship, ethnicity or national origin."

These values still hold today, says Peter Brabeck. In 2002, however, "in order to reflect future challenges without radically altering the existing work ethic and enterprise culture," he decided to update "The Basic Management and Leadership Principles of Nestlé." The new version appeared in 2003 under the title "The Nestlé Management and Leadership Principles." About two-thirds of the original text was retained but there are some notable changes: for example modern management terms like "accountability," "networking," "operational speed" and "result-oriented" are new. Moreover, what is expected of employees has also been revised. Among the important points are:

- responsibility for the wellbeing of consumers and employees
- raising the living standard and quality of life everywhere and for everyone
- mutual respect and tolerance
- pride in the company
- loyalty to and identification with Nestlé
- proactive collaboration beyond conventional internal divisions
- enjoying risk-taking
- sharing knowledge and ideas
- not thinking in isolation
- initiative, with the right to make a mistake but also the willingness to correct it and learn from it.

The focus on shareholder values is more subtly presented than in the first version: "Nestlé requires long-term and successful business development and strives to be a popular investment for long-term shareholders. On the other hand, it does not lose sight of the need to improve short-term results and remains aware that it must make a healthy profit every year."

That Nestlé follows consumer trends but also tries to anticipate them is also new. The Company is also committed to free competition within a clear legal framework and to its "social responsibility," a concept which was not included in the original version.

Brabeck retained striving towards decentralization from the first version, and based the limitations mentioned there on the need for operational efficiency, flexibility and coordination throughout the Company.

Over the years "The Basic Management and Leadership Principles" have taken on the meaning of a kind of "constitution of corporate governance." In the first version in 1997 Peter Brabeck wrote: "These principles express our conviction that, while we must adapt to local and regional conditions, we also have common Nestlé principles which must be universally respected."

Subscribing to these principles became a prerequisite for the appointment of managers from outside the Company. Since 1998, the assessment of a manager's achievements has also reflected the extent to which he or she adheres to these principles.

"Anyone not willing to follow these principles cannot be a part of the company," states the "Nestlé Human Resources Policy" of 2002. Therefore, apart from professional qualifications, attention must be paid to whether a candidate fits the Company's culture.

Business and Personal Leadership

Peter Brabeck has spoken on the subject of leadership, not only within Nestlé but in many public presentations, including one on February

18, 2004 in Geneva, entitled "Business and Personal Leadership." In it, he repeatedly draws parallels between mountain climbing and leading a large company. Here are his main points:

There are two types of mountaineer – the loners who reach the summit on their own, and those who are capable of leading a whole group to the top. A good example of such a team player is Sir Christian John Storey Bonington. As a member of the Norwegian Everest Expedition in 1985, he succeeded in leading eighteen climbers to the top of Everest. Others who tried later failed miserably and twelve members of their expedition died.

If an expedition is to be successful, you must assemble the right team and have a clear idea of your goals and how to achieve them. Only when you are clear about your objectives and how to proceed can you decide what team members with what different skills are needed.

You must therefore find the right people for the right jobs. A competent employee, improperly placed, will be unhappy and never give it his or her all.

Every team needs each member of the team to feel a bond and solidarity with the other members, but there must also be healthy competition between them. It would make no sense to have two team members who always have identical ideas and suggestions, one of the members would be redundant. Even at the top of a company, it makes sense to cultivate a degree of tension and competition. If competition is lacking, you either have to create it, or change the composition of the team.

Of course it all depends on people working together towards the same goals, but there should also be competition in the search for the best solutions. Maintaining the balance in this situation is definitely difficult.

In the history of mountaineering there have always been rigid personalities who on the way to the top have abandoned their partners to die in order to ensure their own success. Anyone climbing Mount Everest will see dead climbers who did not make it back, since no one can bury them or carry them back to the valley.

Strong loners may sometimes be very successful, but they can also do a great deal of harm on an expedition. The same thing applies in business organizations.

What kind of people does Nestlé need at the top today? They must be able to deal with a variety of challenges, such as the increasingly complex markets; they need the ability not only to accept continuous change within the company, but to drive it forward. The pressure of outside competition which employees are exposed to is becoming stronger, and therefore Nestlé needs balanced people. People who, on the one hand can recognize the need for change and the opportunities it offers and are not always looking backward, projecting the past onto the future; but on the other hand, can do what must be done without losing themselves in flights of fancy.

Food, to a great extent, comprises products which are bound up with consumers' emotions and specific cultural values which a Nestlé manager must understand and respect. It is not Nestlé's job to export cultural values and perceptions to other countries, but to provide local markets with products which match their own cultures.

All the top Nestlé managers have lived for several years in other countries and other cultures. The food business is highly local in character and it is therefore important to make it relevant to local conditions.

Whether in the mountains or in an organization, everything depends on a team striking the right balance between the members' skills, competition and cooperation; it is important for them to look after each other because only then can they survive as a group.

Today, teams must take into consideration employees' expectations of their work, while also being able to cope with a growing mass of information. The quantity of irrelevant data in itself is growing incessantly, and not all information adds to the sum of one's knowledge. In order for a team to make the right decisions, data must be turned into knowledge.

As in mountaineering, a point can be reached where different team members take the lead, depending on the situation. Here the most important element is trust. What holds Nestlé employees together is the feeling of social bonding based on strong common values and convictions; but these must be put into practice and adapted to changing situations without losing sight of their underlying principles.

These values are set out in Nestlé's "Management and Leadership Principles" and in the "Corporate Business Principles". Anyone who wants to work for Nestlé must share these values. The worst thing for an organization is when its employees live their professional and personal lives by different value systems.

That other people live by different values and principles is not a problem; they just cannot work for Nestlé. Only where basic values exist can trust be created. Trust is not just an internal factor, but must apply in relationships with external business partners and the general public.

Brabeck sees his own example as one of trust. He has no written employment contract with the Company but every year he is confirmed in his post. He trusts the Company to keep its word, so long as he keeps his.

Things are different in the USA where it is customary for lawyers in the Nestlé office to draw up comprehensive contracts, but all these written rules and agreements are pointless if people do not adhere to them. Social responsibility makes for a healthy organization, not rules and regulations which are promptly ignored.

Mistrust and the abuse of trust are very costly. The number of lawyers in the USA has doubled in the last thirty years and now stands at 750,000 – twice as high as in Europe relative to the number of doctors. In the USA there are over 82,000 lawsuits filed per day. The cost of a pacemaker automatically includes $3,000 to provide for possible litigation.

Billions of dollars are spent annually by organizations on personal liability insurance for their CEOs. All these costs arise from mistrust and in most cases are invisible.

Good leadership must not only create trust but also listen, to effectively include the members of a team into the planning process.

We at Nestlé are convinced that a team can never take over the function of a leader; it needs a leader to take responsibility for the team.

What is the responsibility of leadership? It must choose the right people for the team, offer them a vision, allow them to develop, and create a balance. Some parts of an organization are more successful than others, mainly for reasons of timing.

Peter Brabeck remembers that when he first began his professional career, an organization he worked for merged with its competitor from one day to the next. The ice cream vendor who had been his principal competitor in the morning was his partner by the evening. Although they both sold the same products, they had in the past been successful in different ways, because windows of opportunity for certain measures and strategies open and shut at different times.

The same is true for mountaineering expeditions. There is a right moment to push off and if you miss it, one hour later might well be disastrous. The right moment is also extremely important in business life.

In Nestlé there is a conviction that the CEO serves the organization not vice versa. This is called the principle of value-oriented leadership. Authority should be exercised when it improves decisions, not to show who's boss. That is the difference between value-oriented leadership and hierarchical leadership. There's no point worrying and speculating about hypothetical details of the year 2025; more important is to acknowledge today's strong points and plan to carry them through tomorrow. It is pointless to concentrate on analyzing problems for which there is no solution at present, or to be afraid of making mistakes. A skier cannot afford to be afraid of falling or a race-car driver of crashing his car. Anyone who is afraid of making mistakes should not take the job in the first place.

In every interview regarding a potential promotion, the first question asked the employee is: "What is the greatest mistake you have made to date?" If no such mistake is forthcoming, the employee is not promoted, because anyone who has never made a mistake has also never made a big decision which might be to the company's advantage.

An organization must have a dynamic equilibrium: that means balancing growth and profitability, maintaining the core business while simultaneously looking for innovation, overall efficiency and local opportunities, teamwork and individuality, continuity and change.

However this can only succeed if you don't lose your instinct for what is right. Feelings, personal values and ambitions are often more important than intellectual reflection. A person who relies on his own instincts will be able to do the right thing, although there's a bit of luck in everything, which may even be the most important element.

Inspiring leadership in today's global economy

Peter Brabeck gave another ground-breaking speech in February 2009 at the Center for International Business in the Tuck School of Business at Dartmouth, USA, entitled: "Inspiring Leadership in Today's Global Economy." This title combined two important aspects – inspiring leadership as a timeless concept and the present global economy tailor-made for today's challenges.

Looking back on his own career, Peter Brabeck said: "I had to learn how to manage and how to lead. Management and leadership are different, but both are very important. To manage means to be responsible for fulfilling a task, to take responsibility for getting something done. To lead, on the other hand, means to exercise influence, steering and determining both direction and the ensuing activities. There is thus a fundamental difference: managers are those, who do things right, and leaders are those who show the managers the way to do the right things."

When do you need leadership? The answer is quite simple: when the task is so big that you cannot do it alone, and you depend on other people to achieve your targets. The scope of the endeavor has a direct impact on the quality of your leadership style, for if you have a smaller task, the creation of a team might be sufficient. However, if you have to lead 285,000 employees or, like the President of the United States, 300 million people, leadership demands become greater and more complex, but the fundamentals remain the same.

Great leaders always inspire people, by showing them that their aspirations are worthwhile. Leadership is an emotional appeal to the most fundamental human needs: the need to be recognized as important, to distinguish oneself from others, to be needed, to be useful and a part of a successful and rewarding endeavor.

First, the leader must have a value-driven vision, which is clear, comprehensible and desirable. Second, he is responsible for establishing values and standards to guide people's conduct. Third, he must lay the foundations for trust – tolerance, mutual respect, integrity and competence.

Gaining trust is the foundation of inspiring leadership; it is the difference between management and leadership. You can manage a project without trust for some time, but lasting results can only be sustained if you can mobilize forces towards higher goals.

The time element also plays a role in this and is too often overlooked in the context of leadership. Do you want to achieve a short-term goal like winning a battle, or a medium-term goal like winning a war, or do you strive for a long-term goal such as sustainable peace? For each of these goals a different type of leadership and different people are needed.

In the past, leadership of a company was often characterized by military style thinking. People talked about guerrilla tactics and making a killing on the market; for example, the book "The Art of War" by the Chinese general and military strategist Sun-Tzu is often recommended reading for business leaders today.

In the past, teaching, learning and thinking in business organizations was frequently characterized by strong hierarchical structures:

- delegation of tasks versus delegation of responsibilities;
- obedience rather than taking initiative;
- tasks rather than results;
- vertical career paths through a pyramidal structure rather than free information flow and plasma structures.

We should not undervalue the uses and efficiency of such hierarchies; they served in the past to win battles and guide the course of events. But is it the right approach in today's global economy?

This led Brabeck to the second part of his speech, our actual globalized world. He had just returned from the World Economic Forum in Davos, where he had come to the realization that the words 'network' and 'sustainable' both specifically exemplify today's global economy and its challenges. On this subject he said:

"We live in an extremely complex global network, which is becoming more stable and sustainable. Therefore the old management principles are obsolete. They no longer fit the new conditions and would no longer be accepted. What we need today is inspiring leadership for a complex sustainable global network."

New technologies and instant access to information have had an enormous impact on how to organize and run a company. In Nestlé, every major speech of the CEO, every press conference, every shareholders meeting, is transmitted directly via Intranet to all of the more than 285,000 employees all over the world. Information is no longer an instrument of power for the hierarchy; it is to be used to develop values and attitudes.

"At Nestlé we have eliminated job descriptions for certain kinds of tasks, and employees decide how they want to organize their work and how to set priorities in order to achieve their objectives. Pyramidal organization has been replaced by horizontal forms of organization. In our factories, we have only three organizational levels, from the head of the factory down to the workers."

Results-orientation has replaced adherence to process-driven outcomes. It all depends on collecting knowledge and experience and to make this available to the whole organization. Such requirements are of course fundamentally different from those of a hierarchical structure. Networks need less management but more inspiring leadership to achieve results.

Peter Brabeck then described a meeting in 1972 with Gerald Edelman, a Nobel prize-winner for medicine, which had a lasting influence on his views on organizational structures. He asked Edelman why people's behavior is so different, even though the neural networks in the brain are so similar.

Edelman's reply was that the human brain as a system operates selectively. What we learn and how we learn is done by individual choice. The neural connections organize themselves and create new bonds or dissolve old ones, depending on the demands made on the brain.

This became Brabeck's blueprint for Nestlé's future organization, what today he calls a plasma organization. This is a living organism that changes constantly depending on the people and the demands, which interacts with its external environment. Like a brain, the Nestlé organization constantly creates new nodal points and connections.

Today's executives are our organizational nodal points, with stronger or weaker connections as a function of actual requirements. Employees become our allies, who will – in a constantly changing, complex organization, beyond transparency – automatically achieve results.

Brabeck asks: "What about the efficiency and effectiveness of the operation?" Such a high performance culture can only be organized when governed by principles and values. Internally in Nestle, we have the "Nestlé Management and Leadership Principles," and for our relations with the external world, the "Nestlé Corporate Business Principles." By continuous communication from the top down and from the bottom up, the whole organization is aligned with those principles.

"Everyone in Nestlé knows what goals we are pursuing, how we are going about it. Each person knows that the more we work as a team, the more we contribute to reaching our common goal. Naturally such an organizational structure is very challenging for each individual. Uncertainty and stress call for nerves of steel, good health and a sense of humor."

"The leader's job is to integrate everyone into a harmonious whole. Orchestral conductors are also inspiring leaders. The famous Russian conductor Valerie Gergiev, who happens to be a good personal friend of mine, once told me: 'One of the jobs of a conductor is to give the musicians the maximum feeling of freedom. But freedom requires discipline, from the conductor and from the musicians.'"

Therefore, one of the main tasks of the CEO of a successful company is his continuous fight against complacency, the eternal enemy of sustainable success. Don't forget: you are only as good as your next success, not your last one.

Leadership rests on the wise use of power. It is the basis for translating intention into reality. Mankind has the desire to belong to something bigger than oneself. We want to achieve something which we cannot accomplish alone and to pursue joint aims. We seek knowledge and wish to share those fruits with others. It is the task of Inspiring Leadership to create the foundations for others who would take up this challenge.

Act don't react

Looking back, Peter Brabeck-Letmathe considers the following three decisions as his most important while CEO: the branding policy, the strategic transformation of the business into a nutrition, health and wellness company, and the internal restructuring from a large supertanker into a fleet of agile cruisers and speedboats with a supply ship.

Brands and marketing

Even before his official nomination as CEO, Brabeck together with Helmut Maucher, had drawn up and structured the future product strategy, including policies for brands and communications. Maucher considered Brabeck to be a forward thinker, for defining the products required and the appropriate marketing and communication strategy. As early as 1995 Brabeck was in charge of liaison with the media.

Maucher and Brabeck developed a pyramid of brands consisting of 10 worldwide corporate brands, approximately 50 worldwide strategic product brands, 150 regional strategic brands and 700 local strategic brands, together with 7,500 local brands which were mostly confined to an individual country.

Responsibility for the individual brands lay with the respective strategic business units (SBU): depending on the significance of the brand, general management (for worldwide corporate brands), the zone (for worldwide strategic product brands), or the market (for regional strategic brands) had a shared responsibility.

Over time the number of worldwide corporate brands was reduced from ten to six and the brand hierarchy was simplified. Today Nestlé only has two types of brands – Corporate Brands and Range/

Product brands – which can each be used on all three levels, global, regional or local.

Maucher and Brabeck also jointly developed the concept of the popularly positioned products (PPP), offering low-income people highly nutritive and tasty products at reasonable prices while nevertheless generating a profit for Nestlé. These products were brought on the market in both developing and industrialized countries.

Until the end of the 1980s, Nestlé's brands were actually technology brands: Findus for frozen food technology, Maggi for dried food and Herta for refrigerated products. The technology was the main element of the brand. Buitoni was the first time that the brand was primary, after which a variety of technologies was introduced. This was a paradigm shift.

Brabeck had the idea of starting up a "Casa Buitoni" as the cornerstone for the Buitoni brand. In 1989, Nestlé bought the old Buitoni villa in Sansepolcro, Tuscany, from the Buitoni family where Mrs. Giulia Buitoni had founded the business in 1827.

Nestlé created an R&D and public relations center there which still exists today. The overall brand policy was centered on Casa Buitoni, along with a quality guarantee seal which you still see on its products today. This was an extraordinary move for Brabeck from a brand policy standpoint, which got international press coverage.

When Peter Brabeck had developed this strategy for the Buitoni brand, Helmut Maucher asked him to present it to the Chairman's Committee, which was the first time Brabeck came in contact with Rainer Gut and Fritz Gerber. "That was an interesting conversation," remembers Brabeck. Fritz Gerber was particularly interested in the whole brand strategy because he was considering future changes in the pharmaceutical market in connection with Roche and whether branding policy would become more significant.

Later, Fritz Gerber invited Brabeck to join the Board of Roche, and Brabeck became a member of the Finance Committee. However his main tasks were in marketing and formulating a brand strategy for pharmaceuticals.

"He is a visionary with both feet squarely planted on the ground" – Conversation with Fritz Gerber

Fritz Gerber, born 1929, graduated from the University of Berne with a law degree. He began his career at the Trade Division of the Federal Department of Economic Affairs (now known as SECO) in Berne, where among other duties, he became a member of the delegation which prepared Switzerland's entry into the GATT.

In 1958, he joined the Zurich Insurance Company (now Zurich Financial Services) where he was appointed General Manager in 1969, Chairman of the Management Board in 1974, and Chairman of the Board of Directors and CEO in 1977. In 1991 he stepped down as CEO but continued to serve as Chairman of the Board of Directors until 1995 and has been Honorary Chairman since that time.

In addition to his role with Zurich Insurance Company, in 1978 Gerber began service as Chairman of the Board of Directors and CEO of F. Hoffmann-La Roche AG (now Roche Holding AG).

In 1998 he stepped down as Roche CEO, remaining on as Chairman of the Board of Directors until 2001, member of the Board of Directors until 2004, and Honorary Chairman of the Board since 2001.

He has served on the boards of several other companies, including among others IBM and Credit Suisse for several years, and from 1981 to 2001 he served as the Vice-Chairman of the Board of Directors at Nestlé. He is the founder and Honorary Chairman of the Fritz Gerber Foundation for talented young people, and is also involved in the field of music. Among his other leadership activities, Fritz Gerber served as the Chairman of the Paul Sacher Foundation until 2006, and was a Member of the Executive Committee of the Lucerne Festival until 2004. He is an Honorary Doctor of Philosophy and Natural Sciences at the University of Basel.

The conversation with Fritz Gerber might well not have happened at all, because of a case of laryngitis, however he was so committed to making a contribution to this book that he decided to do his best to speak. He was pleased when he found that not only did his voice improve the longer he spoke, but so did his mood.

What struck Fritz Gerber first and foremost in Peter Brabeck was his marketing experience, and the fact that in many respects Brabeck's outlook was quite different from his own. Over the years, they have developed an excellent cooperative and close relationship. Gerber, whose background was in finance, freely admits that he learned a lot about marketing from Brabeck. They would usually see each other at the monthly meetings of the Nestlé Chairman's Committee.

Fritz Gerber found that he really appreciated both Helmut Maucher's and Peter Brabeck's ability to tackle problems in a very direct way rather than getting tangled up in formalities. Therefore he was overjoyed when Peter Brabeck accepted the invitation to become a member of the Roche Board of Directors in 2000. In this role Brabeck was a forceful complement to Fritz Gerber's successor, Franz B. Humer, and thoroughly enjoyed encountering new and different points of view.

Fritz Gerber describes Peter Brabeck as a visionary, although he is hesitant to use this term because usually visionaries do not have their feet squarely planted on the ground; this absolutely never happened in Brabeck's case. As Gerber puts it, Brabeck was not one of the "non-sense managers," rather he kept ambitious and realistic goals in mind. At the same time, he had an eye and instinct for future developments. His intellectual strengths were combined with his ability to communicate easily with colleagues on all levels and to strike the right tone. Gerber emphasizes that this gift is rare.

In Gerber's opinion, Nestlé went in the right direction when it set out to emphasize wellness, health and nutrition, but he laments that companies in industrialized countries should have adopted this attitude towards nutrition much earlier.

Gerber gives Nestlé high marks for contributing so much to this awareness, but notes that it has a conflict of interest in some areas. For example, Nestlé sells sweets for children, the benefits of which are questionable. However, cognizant of this conflict, they have invested heavily in research and development. Discussion concerning healthy nutrition can become very interesting when the contrasting positions of a food company and a pharmaceutical company clash.

Fritz Gerber still remembers quite well the public debate when Peter Brabeck was to take on the double mandate at Nestlé. At the time, Gerber supported this and as a consequence had, like many others, been heavily criticized. In the USA such combined appointments were common and very successful, Gerber noted, but in Switzerland people had become unnecessarily embroiled in heated discussions about this, and, in the Nestlé case, hung up on formalities.

Every company has to find the best leadership structure, given its particular situation. Making clear who has responsibility for what is of the highest importance; there is never any reason to spread responsibility out so broadly that ultimately no one holds any responsibility at all.

Referring to Peter Brabeck's hobbies of mountaineering, flying and motorcycling, Fritz Gerber said, "He loves taking risks but fortunately he knows how to deal with it," noting that it is better to have someone who is able to manage risks than someone who just tries to avoid them.

The fact that Peter Brabeck was not a Swiss citizen was no longer a problem for the Swiss. Ultimately Brabeck won people over with his character, striking appearance and manner. Fritz Gerber muses that many Swiss would like to climb mountains or do military service with Brabeck, because they know that they can always count on him.

Blueprint for the Future

In June 1997, immediately after taking his post, Brabeck put forward his first "Blueprint for the Future" at a meeting of the Market Heads in Vevey; here he elaborated his ideas for Nestlé's future. This paper was distributed to all of Nestlé's employees worldwide. Further blueprints by Peter Brabeck would follow on a regular basis at eighteen-month intervals.

Brabek wrote of his decision to put aside grand visions and concentrate pragmatically on Nestlé's strengths. As the world's leading food producer, Nestlé was better positioned to recognize opportunities for the future than any of its main competitors. It was essential to concentrate on the numerous existing ideas and plans which needed to be adapted, strengthened or renewed.

Brabeck was also opposed to complacency, which he described as the greatest enemy of success. In his opinion there were no saturated markets, just satiated managers. He warned against accepting simple solutions like shutting a factory down rather than taking up the challenge of creating new products to make that plant profitable again.

Finally he raised the issue of whether the policy of aggressive outward expansion was compatible with successful internal growth and announced that in the future the main focus would once again be internal growth.

Brabeck set himself the target of achieving an internal volume growth rate of four percent and a simultaneous and continual improvement of the EBITDA margin (earnings before interest, taxes, depreciation and amortization). Later he set the target for organic growth at five to six percent.

Peter Brabeck defined the most important internal growth field to be nutrition, in other words a healthy diet. His first action as CEO was to set up a business division for this and he assumed direct responsibility for it. In 2006, Nestlé Nutrition was turned into an autonomous, globally-led division.

To strengthen Nestlé's competitiveness on a sustainable level he formulated a four-pronged strategy, the elements of which were not new but which were to receive greater attention. These were:

1. To achieve operational efficiency and consequently a reduction in production and administration costs.
2. To drive forward product Innovation and Renovation, both in terms of taste and nutritional quality, for products which had achieved above-average scores in the so-called 60/40 comparative tests. All Nestlé products were to be tested and only those which

were preferred over the competition's products by at least 60 percent of the testers would be introduced onto the market or receive marketing support.

3. To increase the consumer product availability on the principle that all products should be accessible "whenever, wherever, however" the consumer wants them.
4. To improve communication with consumers in order to show the Nestlé brands in their best possible light, both emotionally and functionally.

From super-tanker to agile fleet

Brabeck made clear that the Nestlé product portfolio had to be continually adapted to reach his ambitious targets. In this regard he followed three basic principles:

1. The Renovation of traditional brands and products which still make up the largest part of the turnover and profit. These include instant coffee, milk drinks and other powdered drinks, culinary products and chocolate.
2. Expansion of faster-growing segments. Here Brabeck gives priority to three product categories: water, ice cream and pet food. He considers the strategic integration of these three new areas to be a particularly important decision because Nestlé is global market leader in each of these product categories. Also included in these fast growing areas are all products which benefit from the increase in eating out and the trend towards smaller and more frequent meals.
3. Participation in and strengthening of growth areas and exploring new business opportunities. Brabeck subsequently sold the business divisions in which Nestlé's specific knowledge contributed little to value creation, and looked for new product categories. These include performance diets, medical and nutritional services and products for weight management, product lines with specific

nutritional properties and specific services which help consumers achieve their personal nutritional goals.

Brabeck believes that of the three most important decisions he made as CEO, the second one, the strategic conversion from food manufacturer to a nutrition, health and wellness company, required the third one as a prerequisite, namely the internal restructuring of the business.

In March 2000, Peter Brabeck introduced the GLOBE Project (Global Business Excellence) – a far-reaching organizational transformation process whose implementation phase finished at the end of 2006. To this day, he is convinced that without this restructuring it would no longer have been possible to efficiently manage a company of this size and complexity.

The super-tanker Nestlé was to be transformed into a fleet of agile cruisers and high-speed patrol boats which would be led by a strategic flagship – the head office in Vevey – and supported by regional and global supply ships.

GLOBE was the means which enabled the transformation in the first place. It was neither a pure IT project nor a cost-reduction program but contained elements of both. The basic idea lay in leveraging the size of the Group effectively as an asset in a fast-changing environment and to strengthen its core through coordination and amalgamation in order to be more competitive at a global level and to combine complexity with operational efficiency. The introduction of three main programs put these basic ideas into effect:

1. Best practices;
2. Data standards and data management;
3. Standardized information systems and technologies.

"We split the company up into its individual business processes, which numbered over eight hundred," reports Brabeck, "beginning with the initial approach by the salesman to a customer through when the goods finally reach the individual consumer. In between, there were procurement, production, distribution, marketing, financial management, controlling and personnel. We then chose the best practices for each business process and communicated these to all employees worldwide for global application. Finally we put the whole thing back together. It was a mammoth task and the risk was very great, which took the share price down for a while," Brabeck recalls. "That was because no company – and certainly not one as big as Nestlé – had ever managed to deconstruct the business processes from A to Z, before building them back up again. There was a danger that, in the process, we might paralyze the company for a brief time or even longer if the building blocks didn't precisely fit back together again. Other companies had already tried something similar – for example, in the case of an American competitor, this resulted in the company's not being able to make deliveries for two months. This example probably haunted the analysts. The project cost three billion Swiss francs and employed over 2,000 people full time for over six years. It wasn't exactly easy."

Brabeck describes the choice of Project Leader as the most crucial element. He chose Chris Johnson, a young American who had made a positive impression on him for some time. Wherever he worked, in the USA, in Japan, as Market Head in Taiwan or in the water business, he had been highly innovative and had introduced new business processes.

"He was no IT specialist, but was a highly innovative businessman and a very strong project leader. I brought him into senior management immediately, making the importance we attached to the project very clear to the outside world, and I was also heavily involved.

"I always said that the success or failure of GLOBE would be my biggest legacy to the Company. Without GLOBE we would not have the advantage that we have today: the combination of complexity and efficiency. I am probably being generous to say that in the beginning, 80 percent in the organization were against the project and 20 percent for it. Then we really worked to explain the concept and make it a key priority; had we not done so it would probably not have gone through. I bore the entire responsibility for this project and had it gone wrong my time as CEO would probably have come to an end. GLOBE was a hot topic for a time in the business world; many entrepreneurs were interested in it and much was written about it in the media."

In January 2004, GLOBE began to be implemented in about 80 percent of Nestlé's food and beverages businesses. Over 100,000 users, 500 factories, 400 distribution centers and more than 300 sales offices began to take advantage of the new opportunities. As a result of GLOBE, Nestlé's employees collaborated in a more disciplined way and gathered and exchanged more information which helped the coordination between the various departments involved in decision-making.

Cleaning up Nestlé's database revealed that over 50 percent of the data on the approximately six million items, customers and suppliers was either outdated or duplicated and of that, a further 35 percent contained errors or inaccuracies. These high percentages might horrify a layman; however experts know that such figures are by no means unusual in large companies undertaking this kind of database cleanup.

Today, Nestlé concretely knows that approximately 120,000 different items are sold of which 25,000 are exported abroad. In total there are more than 300 global standards which facilitate reporting, shipments between individual markets and commercial decision processes.

Although it is still difficult to quantify GLOBE's success, all those involved know beyond any doubt that, without GLOBE, neither the organizational changes nor the improvement in financial performance could have been achieved.

Democratizing information

Communication with customers, shareholders, the public and Nestlé employees worldwide ranks very high among Peter Brabeck's priorities, so he drew up a blueprint and made it available to the entire organization on his first day as CEO – the first CEO in Nestlé's history to do such a thing.

It was important to him that every one in the company down to the employees on the shop floor should know exactly what he wanted to do and why. Brabeck also recognized that going directly to the Markets and talking directly to the people is essential. During his time in South America he says he was very dissatisfied with the communication policy. A Market Heads Conference took place only once every two years in Vevey, to which the most important CEOs from different countries were invited to report on their plans and priorities.

"Our boss in Chile spent a week in Vevey," Brabeck remembers. "Naturally we were all interested in whatever was in store for us, what decisions were made and how they would affect us. But he was the only one who knew what had been said.

"After his return, he waited until the next General Managers' meeting to brief them. It took two months before my supervisor at the time, who was responsible for Savory ice cream, came to tell us what had happened in Vevey.

"The problem by then was that the personal views of both the CEO and the General Managers permeated the information to such a degree that its original meaning was barely comprehensible.

"As a result of this experience, communication became a great challenge for me from the start, because when I was planning to make changes I had to be sure that the employees in the local market would understand those changes, otherwise I could not have executed my plans.

"This task has been made much easier for me because of the enormous advances in communication technology. First we installed the Intranet, which was a revolution; all Nestlé employees worldwide now had the opportunity to examine my blueprint. Since then CEO meetings, press conferences and even Annual General Meetings have been webcast live and every employee can participate in them directly.

Now the chauffeur and the employee on the shop floor in Düsseldorf know just as much as the Market Head in Germany. All that is required is to log on to the computer and you can follow everything. That was the democratization of information.

"Previously information was a tool of power: I know, but you know nothing and I decide how much to tell you. Today a Manager can no longer tell his workforce 'those upstairs' made this or that demand, because everyone is now able to see for themselves what was said."

Gap creation instead of Benchmarking

When Peter Brabeck became CEO, benchmarking was a common practice throughout the entire industry. This meant comparing your own company with the top companies in the field and trying to attain "best in class." "That is not very innovative," says Brabeck. "We were already best in class under Helmut Maucher, so who should we be comparing ourselves with?"

Brabeck then decided on the next move: benchbreaking, which means doing everything to create the largest possible gap between Nestlé and its competitors. He introduced the 'gap creation' model. "We must not look back, but distance ourselves from the competition and create an artificial gap between us and our competitors in all we do. Through such 'gap creation' we can progress faster and farther than the competition."

Brabeck explains: "Of course benchmarking is simpler, but the difference with benchbreaking is analogous to the American runner at the Olympic Games, who always ran ten meters in front of everyone else; he didn't benchmark himself against his competitors nor did he look to see whether he was at the same level as the second, third or fourth runner, but he just ran his own race. Naturally this way of doing things is much more demanding but it makes all the difference.

The last Bivouac on Aconcagua (2008).

The first Carinthian Hindu Kush expedition (1967).

In the Swiss Alps.

Landing on the Trient glacier.

Autographed photo from General Chuck Yeager, the first man to break the sound barrier.

Brabeck in an F-18 fighter jet before takeoff.

On the ground with President Salvador Allende (1972).

Marketing in Chile: the Kukulina-Show (1974).

Market Head in Venezuela (1983).

Succeeding Helmut Maucher as CEO (1997).

Silvia Pfenniger

With Rainer E. Gut.

With the new CEO Paul Bulcke (2008).

Mr. and Mrs. Fritz Gerber with Mr. and Mrs. Peter Brabeck-Letmathe.

Silvia Pfenniger

With Walter B. Kielholz on the occasion of Sechseläuten, a traditional Zurich Spring celebration.

Silvia Pfenniger

With Swiss Federal President Doris Leuthard at the World Economic Forum in Davos.

Silvia Pfenniger

With Federal Councillor Pascal Couchepin.

With Maestro Valery Gergiev in Salzburg.

At the Salzburg Festival with Festival President Helga Rabl-Stadler.

Decorated by Austrian Chancellor Wolfgang Schüssel.

In discussion with Ernesto Zedillo Ponce de Léon, President of Mexico 1994–2000.

Peter Brabeck visiting a school he founded in Venezuela.

Creating Shared Value by protecting coffee plants in Mexico.

Creating Shared Value by creating a milk district in India.

Creating Shared Value by nutrition education in Korea.

Nestlé's Creating Shared Value Advisory Board, seated from left to right: Kraisid Tontisirin, Michael Porter (Harvard Business School), Peter Brabeck, Joachim von Braun, Venkatesh Mannar; standing from left to right: Paul Bulcke, Robert Black, Irving Rosenberg, Jeffrey D. Sachs, Robert L. Thompson, John Elkington, Niels Christiansen.

World Economic Forum/swiss-image.ch

Kofi Annan, General Secretary of the UNO 1997–2006, and Nobel Peace Prize winner in 2001.

With Amir Dossal, Director of the United Nations Office for Partnerships in New York (on the left in the picture).

At the Creating Shared Value Forum in New York in 2009.

World Economic Forum/swiss-image.ch

With German Chancellor Angela Merkel and WEF-Founder Klaus Schwab in Davos.

World Economic Forum/swiss-image.ch

In discussion with Chinese Prime Minister Wen Jiabao.

World Economic Forum/swiss-image.ch

With Klaus Schwab, Federal Councillor Hans-Rudolf Merz and Russian President Vladimir Putin at the WEF in Davos.

With his wife Bernadette and Maestro Gergiev.

His three children Andrès, Carolina, and Nicolas.

Fanny, Carolina, and Daphne Brabeck-Letmathe.

With his children and his sister Gerda Piccinini.

Bernadette and Peter Brabeck-Letmathe.

With his granddaughter Clara.

With his grandson Léo.

"The Nestlé model was at that time a gap creation. When I first became CEO I was asked what my priority was – increasing turnover or profit. My response was that I would turn 'either/or' into 'and' – gap creation vis-a-vis our competitors." This concept was new, it derived from Brabeck's basic stance – don't rest on your laurels, continually open up new strategic flanks which place you ahead of the competition, forcing them to play catch-up.

Brabeck says that the Nestlé principle of "whenever, wherever, however" is a further example of gap creation. Competitors were concentrating on growth primarily by selling their products through international retail chains, but this was not good enough for Brabeck. One major competitor was making over 50 percent of its turnover through its five biggest clients. "I said I don't want to do that, I want our products to be available everywhere – whenever, wherever, however." Today 20 percent of Nestlé's turnover comes from the ten largest international retailers. "So naturally we are much better protected if there are problems with one retailer."

In the field of marketing, Nespresso is a typical example of gap creation. Brabeck had decided to sell the roast coffee business because he was tired of fighting competitors over whether a cup of coffee cost 6.5 centimes or 7 centimes. A cup of Nespresso today costs 50 centimes.

"From the start we bought the best coffee in the world for Nespresso – only one to two percent of coffee production worldwide meets Nespresso's quality requirements – and that is still the case," says Brabeck, adding that while this is extremely important, it is even more important for the consumer's individual cup of Nespresso to be freshly roasted.

The coffee for each individual cup must be vacuum-packed immediately. When coffee is taken out of a kilo package the aroma fades relatively quickly, but a Nespresso capsule is only opened when the cup of coffee is made and so its aroma and freshness are retained in every cup. That is why the coffee is so delicious.

The technology of preparing Nespresso enters into this too. The capsule is not cut open; the aluminum foil opens itself under high pressure and steam not water reaches the coffee first. That method is what makes Nespresso espresso and not just ordinary coffee. The hot steam opens the pores of the coffee and then the water follows. "That is what makes the coffee so original and that is the reason for its success. If we did not have this superb quality, even George Clooney and the best advertising could not help," Brabeck stressed.

However the greatest example of gap creation says Brabeck, was the idea of changing from a food industry to create a new industrial category of nutrition, health and wellness, and to position ourselves as the undisputed market leader. The most successful food company in the world was thus transformed into the world's leading research-driven nutrition, health and wellness company.

"Thus, we established ourselves in a new arena and left the competition behind.

"Now they are following us, take for instance Danone which now is also a nutrition, health and wellness company, but on a much smaller scale than Nestlé."

Naturally the major part of Nestlé's turnover, currently 83 percent, still comes from the food business, but Nestlé is constantly working on transforming its food products into products with a higher nutritional value. In addition, the scope for customer service and consultation is growing. Through specific acquisitions – for example Jenny Craig, Novartis Medical Nutrition and Gerber – Nestlé is already the undisputed market leader in the field of "specialized nutrition."

One important prerequisite for transforming Nestlé into a nutrition, health and wellness company was a restructuring of its research and development activities. Today Nestlé's research is concentrated on eight health-promoting fields, each with a vast potential for opening up new business activities.

Nestlé Nutrition's research is working on several projects which are of prime importance for an aging population. Other products reduce the side effects of chemotherapy or radiotherapy on cancer sufferers, and many other products simply help to improve the quality of life for all consumers, for example through strengthening the immune system.

Nestlé research is not only developing new products and ingredients but also new processes such as extrusion technology, in which Nestlé has decades of experience and which is used in breakfast cereals, energy bars, pasta and pet food.

Out of this research came a process for producing low-calorie ice cream through low temperature freezing. As there was no existing business framework for this, Nestlé sold it to the American company Dreyer's, in which it had a minority holding; when Nestlé later acquired a majority interest, this successful process returned home.

Earlier structural changes had been made in the Research and Development department, so that when Brabeck took the helm as CEO full scale reform could begin. His objective was to bring research, production and marketing closer together. The first step was to merge R&D with the production, technical and environmental departments under the management of Rupert Gasser.

As a result, research was concentrated in only a few locations, and research projects were reduced in number in order to shorten the time lag before a new product was launched. Finally, Brabeck created Product Technology Centers, where the overall authority for everything from initial research to production and packaging was combined.

The idea of a Wellness Company

Peter Brabeck says that he spent his first two or three years as CEO primarily focused on introducing the Nestlé Model and strengthening the three major new product areas of ice cream, water and pet care, in part through acquisitions. At the same time he simplified product lines, for instance by divesting the tomato and roasted coffee divisions.

In parallel, Brabeck was working on Nestlé's future. In 2000 he presented a document entitled "The Wellness Company" to the

Board of Directors. His vision was a wellness company resting on three pillars: Food, Pharmaceuticals and Personal Care.

Peter Brabeck saw that the possibilities for future growth in the traditional food industry were very limited. Greater growth was only possible through making further acquisitions or through steering a new course towards higher value products largely based on research and development. He envisaged products in segments of the market which were less standardized and aimed in particular at wealthier consumers.

Given that the population is aging and still wants to be fit and healthy in old age, Brabeck hit on the idea of holistic wellness which he was convinced would increase in importance in the future. Wellness begins with a diet suited to the various stages of life, one which has a positive impact on both physical and mental wellbeing. At any age nutrition can help prevent illness, but holistic wellness encompasses much more than that.

This is where the cosmetic and personal-care industry comes in. Its growth rate far exceeds that of the food industry and customers do not react so sensitively to pricing. It is now gaining in importance in supermarkets and larger food stores.

In recent years, there has been pressure on the pharmaceutical industry to lower prices, which did not come from the consumer but from government agencies. In wealthier countries there is a trend towards so-called lifestyle medicines. Since only two-thirds of known diseases can currently be treated effectively, development of new pharmaceutical products can be guaranteed to grow.

So far the three branches of food and beverages, cosmetics and personal care, and pharmaceuticals have been operating independently of each other, according to their own rules. With the increasing desire for wellness, consumers are beginning to compare these industries and sales channels for these products are beginning to overlap.

Peter Brabeck floated the idea of a wellness company which would combine the products in these three sectors, thus utilizing the existing synergies in research and development and in marketing and branding policy, as well as in the sales organization. A company in this sector would have a high growth potential for turnover and profit. He said that Nestlé should take this opportunity to place itself in the lead in this new business and to develop slowly but steadily from being the world leader in food and beverages to being the initiator and market leader of this new global business.

In Brabeck's view, the main factors will be timing, step-by-step creation of a platform as the basis for the future, the search for suitable partners for research, sales and marketing, and lastly the ability to overcome a certain opposition from the financial markets which would prefer the investor to choose only one of the three fields.

In 2000, Brabeck was already proposing some practical initiatives for Nestlé's progress towards becoming a wellness company:

- Reorienting corporate communications;
- Nutrition to become a clear strategic priority, especially performance and clinical nutrition, along with the appropriate acquisitions;
- Strengthened collaboration with L'Oréal;
- Adapting basic research, including in collaboration with pharmaceutical companies, in order to situate the importance of nutritional research relative to diagnostics, genomics and genetics;
- Thorough examination of the over-the-counter market (non-prescription medications), to become familiar with the regulations of this sector;
- Setting up a venture capital fund to support promising start-ups;
- Further analysis of the opportunities for acquisitions and mergers, especially in the over-the-counter market, to strengthen overall strategy.

When the Board of Directors wanted him to rethink this concept, Brabeck and a consultant went through his model in detail oncc more: "We analyzed each of these businesses and the models behind them."

He came to the conclusion that the pharmaceutical sector needed a completely different business model from that of food and personal care and that it would therefore have no future in Nestlé. "I had included the pharmaceutical business because at the time I believed that diagnostics were the connecting link between these three product categories," he recalls. "Today I am still of the same opinion, but I know that I don't need my own pharmaceutical company for this."

Brabeck is convinced that all three areas will, in the long run, develop towards personalization – that is, the creation of personalized nutrition, personalized medicine and personalized personal care. To achieve this, you need strong diagnostics but not your own pharmaceutical company.

Once Brabeck had discarded the idea of the pharmaceutical company, the Board of Directors agreed with his plan. "So we laid the foundations for the first step from a food company to a nutrition, health and wellness company."

You can see further from the summit

A year before he became delegate of Nestlé's Board of Directors, Peter Brabeck-Letmathe gave a speech in Austria in his home province of Carinthia on the subject of success:

"Personal success is a field with big differences between appearance and reality. People's imagination and fascination with personality hugely distort the real person. The dictionary gives two definitions of success. One is gaining power, fame or fortune; the other achieving positive results, a happy outcome of purposeful striving.

"I feel closer to the latter definition because if wealth had been my objective, I would have become a private entrepreneur supplying Nestlé, which pays its suppliers very well. If I wanted fame, I would have become an actor or a musician, and politics would have been a more suitable route to power."

Peter Brabeck defines personal success as a series of positive results, which includes the correct assessment of what is possible, and the pleasure of attaining it. A mountaineer should increase his or her pace gradually up to the first high peak. First you go hiking and enjoy nature. Then after a long hike you come to your first smaller peaks, and delight in the scenic view of a wide and open world. These stages were like the stages of his professional career, from product manager to marketing.

Then came his first experiences in climbing school, the personal challenge of learning something new. Brabeck compares his first major climbing excursions, from an easy ascent to free climbing, to his business experience in Chile – years which were not easy, but rich in experience in all spheres of life.

A mountaineer strives to conquer more difficult and higher peaks, thus his circle of climbing friends gets smaller and the effort expended greater. In his professional life, after Chile came the decisive step back from specialization into the head office.

On Mount Ararat in Turkey, while climbing his first 5,000-meter peak, he learned to appreciate solitude at the top for the first time. And in Quito, Ecuador, at an altitude of 3,000 meters, the loneliness of a CEO first penetrated his consciousness.

On the Tirich Mir expedition in 1967, the first expedition made by Carinthians to the Hindu Kush, he learned to cope with death and disaster. "But even in such situations you have to keep your head up, and orient yourself by the light that exists on every dark horizon, if you look for it," Brabeck emphasizes.

After this experience he says, he was greatly tempted to turn his back on the mountains, to forget and move on. Instead he searched for a new relationship with the mountains – he was no longer interested only in the menacing ridge, the ledge that blocked the path or the steepest ice field, but also in standing before a gentle vista, lying in a fragrant mountain meadow, saying a prayer at the summit, and friendly encounters in remote mountain huts.

In his professional work, he went from Ecuador to the milder climate of Venezuela, where the difficult nationalization negotiations and the complex political situation required empathy and adaptability in order to hold one's own socially.

Today, mountains are "no longer challenges but faithful friends, playmates for my ever-shrinking leisure time," says Brabeck. On the other hand mountains are a standing warning, not to overestimate oneself or take oneself too seriously. As a mountaineer you know that as you climb, you must already be planning the descent, and that a mountain adventure is only a success when you return to the valley safe and sound.

The Tirich Mir Expedition – a crucial experience

In 1967, before he embarked on his professional career, Peter Brabeck joined an expedition to the 7,700-meter Tirich Mir peak in the Karakoram range of the Himalayas, which his mountaineer friend Hans Thomasser was organizing for a group from Carinthia. Peter Brabeck described his experience in a conversation reported in Georg Bachler's book, "Peak performance – borderline experiences and principles of success in management and extreme mountain climbing."

The young men had no money for a flight to Pakistan so they bought an old VW bus and loaded it with the minimum equipment needed. The budget for the whole expedition was 5,000 dollars, most of which was spent on the vehicle. One company donated the material which their mothers sewed into tents; a small business gave them all anoraks.

On the way to Tirich Mir the group climbed the 5,165-meter Mount Ararat, the highest mountain in Turkey. This was Brabeck's first climb above 5,000 meters. When they arrived in Pakistan they could not afford the cost of the climb but were allowed into the valley to photograph flowers at 5,500 meters. No one had ever set foot in this valley before.

The group was accompanied to the base camp at the foot of the mountain by eighteen porters. When the porters turned back, the Austrian group made the first attempt on Tirich Mir via a wall of ice and rock which led directly to the summit. Since they no longer had porters, the climb was quite a challenge. First they had to test out a suitable route by climbing it without their packs, return, and then repeat the climb with a full pack.

Ultimately, two members had to turn back for health reasons; one had a toothache and the other was running a fever. At 6,700 meters, heavy snow slowed the three remaining members of the expedition and their provisions were running out. They realized that at most they had only enough food for two people.

They drew lots. The two winners would climb to the summit and the loser – which turned out to be Peter Brabeck – would have to turn back. He never saw his two friends again. He climbed the mountain again and again, searching for them again and again. It was not until two years later that one of their rucksacks was found.

A passion for mountaineering

"I grew up in the mountains," says Brabeck. So his passion for climbing is not surprising. His parents took him on short trips into the mountains where at age ten he was already hanging on a rope. Later he and his friend Hans Thomasser went bicycling in the Julian Alps, each trip more challenging than the last.

The powerful fascination that mountains have always had for Brabeck drew him to the South American Andes. When asked about borderline experiences during a climb, he stressed that the Tirich Mir expedition was not one of these: he did not quit before reaching the summit, but drew the short straw – since there was not enough food for three people – and had to turn back.

However, he has broken off climbs that had too high a risk. On the Matterhorn (4,478 meters) he was overtaken by a snowstorm at 4,200 meters. His guide was surprised that he wanted to give up so near the top, but Brabeck thought the risk too great. One year later he came back and scaled the Matterhorn. To him the climbing experience has always been much more important than reaching the top.

When asked who he admires as role models, Peter Brabeck names his predecessor Helmut Maucher, a climber, and two orchestra conductors. He values Maucher for his perspicacity, and for always making up his own mind. He could convince you and sell his ideas.

His second model is Sir Christian John Storey Bonington, the British mountaineer born in 1934, who made nineteen expeditions to the Himalayas, four of them to Everest. He led the first successful climb of the southwest wall.

Bonington is one of the most versatile professional mountaineers of the 20th century. He wrote 15 books about his experiences. He was knighted in 1996, and in 2005 became Chancellor of Lancaster University. What Brabeck admires about Bonington is that he was probably the first ever to take an entrepreneurial view of climbing. He divided the members of his expeditions into groups and gave them different tasks: one group for the important functions at the base, a second for the technical aspects and then there were the extreme climbers. This group he held back as much as possible to save their energies and prepare the assault on the summit.

Brabeck finds this kind of leadership interesting, and it was on his initiative that Sir Chris Bonington was given the opportunity to speak about his mountaineering experiences and his concept of leadership at the 2004 World Economic Forum in Davos.

His revolutionary concept of mountaineering impressed Peter Brabeck, because it presented a paradigm shift: most well-known climbers like Reinhold Messner are loners, but Bonington took the step from individual to group efforts, making mountaineering into a triumph of team work.

Alongside his passion for climbing, Peter Brabeck developed a love of music early in life. His grandfather was a composer and also sang at the Berlin Opera. Brabeck dreamt of becoming a conductor, but had to accept that he did not have enough talent. He has given up playing the piano.

A conductor with entrepreneurial sensitivity

Brabeck values the impressive conducting, but especially the "incredible entrepreneurial sensitivity," of Valery Gergiev, conductor of the Mariinsky Theater in St Petersburg.

Gergiev was born in 1953 and studied at the Leningrad Conservatory. In 1977, he won the Herbert von Karajan Conducting Competition in Berlin and on his return to Russia became assistant to Yuri

Temirkanov at the Mariinsky Theater, where he made his debut with Prokofiev's "War and Peace." In 1988, he was named artistic director and has been General Manager of the theater since 1996.

It was Gergiev's goal from the start to make the Mariinsky Theater the best "enterprise in the business." Brabeck admires him for having the theater completely rebuilt in record time raising the money for it largely on his own initiative. He raised money from private individuals all over the world and ultimately managed to convince the government in Moscow to invest in the theater.

Claudio Abbado is the second conductor whom Brabeck names as one of his role models. Nestlé had long been the principal sponsor of the Lucerne Festival. When the administrator Michael Haefliger and Claudio Abbado jointly proposed forming an international Lucerne Festival Orchestra, Brabeck agreed to be its founding sponsor.

The orchestra consists of the best soloists in the world who meet in Lucerne for two weeks every year. Under the direction of Claudio Abbado, they have opened the Lucerne Festival every summer since 2003 with three concerts, which Brabeck is convinced are "probably among the best performances in the world." The Lucerne Festival Orchestra does worldwide tours, and has performed in Tokyo, New York, Vienna and Rome.

To make clear to his fellow managers what an orchestra and the senior management have in common, Brabeck did something extraordinary in one of his first meetings as CEO. He invited a symphony orchestra to Montreux and sat all the Nestlé managers next to the musicians, so they could experience how an orchestra works and the importance of the conductor.

A conductor has an absolutely clear idea of how a piece of music should sound. He needs the whole team. The role of the boss is to give direction and to help the members of the individual team. As outstanding as a soloist may be, a conductor is needed for the group to become a success. Brabeck wanted to show that even the best soloists will only become a world-class orchestra if all strive towards the same end, which requires a high degree of discipline from both the conductor and the orchestra. That's the only way to give an orchestra a sense of freedom, says Brabeck.

"He is a truly courageous person" – Conversation with Helga Rabl-Stadler

Helga Rabl-Stadler was born in 1948; after studying law, journalism and political science in Salzburg, where she earned a doctorate in law, she worked as an economic and domestic affairs journalist for "Die Presse," "Wochenpresse" and "Kurier." From 1983 to 2007, she was co-owner of the Resmann fashion house in Salzburg.

From 1983 to 1990, and again in November 1994, she was a member of parliament for the Austrian People's Party (Österreichische Volkspartei) and from 1991 to 1995 Deputy Federal Chairman of the party. The Salzburg Chamber of Trade and Industry elected her Vice President in 1985 and President in 1988.

On January 26, 1995, she became President of the Salzburg Festival and retired from her political posts. In 2004 her contract was extended to 2014.

" ***You can probably guess why Peter Brabeck sent me to you for an interview about him?***

Peter Brabeck likes people who speak their minds. He does so too, and likes to find exact right words. I think I've entertained him a few times along those lines. I first met him in 1995 through the former Nestlé Chairman, Helmut Maucher. Of course Brabeck, who looks like a movie star, makes an immediate impression on a woman.

We hit it off right away and over the years became good friends. The wonderful thing about my position as President of the Salzburg Festival is that much of my work feels more like a hobby.

Of course it can be hard work to say the right thing at the right time to convince a sponsor that his or her money is well invested. That was and is particularly challenging with Peter Brabeck, because he can see through a weak argument immediately; the inevitable questions follow which you can't gloss over with a few polite words.

He has always questioned the value of being a sponsor; he did not simply want to continue just out of tradition. He always questions whether traditions are still valid and that's very important for a business.

There's a very nice saying by Gustav Mahler, the famous Austrian composer: "Tradition is the spreading of fire and not the veneration of ashes." For both Mahler and Peter Brabeck, tradition isn't something dead to be conserved. Tradition is the good he wants to pass on. In the history of a firm, it is the fire which marks success, not just a repetition of what came before.

There is another proverb that applies equally to Peter Brabeck. It's from the famous novel "The Leopard" by Giovanni di Lampedusa: "If you want to keep everything the same, you must change everything." "Seizing change as the only way to stay on top" is typical of Brabeck. That's very un-Austrian. Austrians usually see change as an unfair burden imposed upon them by Fate, and fail to recognize that only change can open the door to improvement. Of course, change can also mean change for the worse, but as a creative person I prefer to believe in change for the better.

One last quotation, this one from Carl Amery: "Risk is the bow wave of success." Without risk we can't achieve anything. Peter Brabeck is a shining example of this, both in his private and in his professional life. He is an extreme sportsman. That suits him very well. He seeks out danger in order to emerge a stronger person.

Your description was probably the most concise of all the people I interviewed. Many people seemed to shy away from detail.

First of all, I'm not so cautious, which has always served me well in life. But you have to keep in mind that most of the people you interviewed, at least those I am aware of, are his competitors in some way or another. Admittedly, not competitors in terms of products, but as successful managers. Which naturally brings up for them: Is he better than I am? Is there something he does better than I? He's so good looking and clever too – is he more successful?

You're right, Brabeck succeeded both Helmut Maucher and Rainer Gut.

I know them both well, value them as outstanding business personalities and have a great deal to thank them for. It was Helmut Maucher who recognized the affinity between Nestlé and the Festival: "A shared passion for quality." It was Rainer E. Gut who together with Helmut Maucher, convinced Credit Suisse to sponsor the Salzburg Festival.

Of course, it's not easy to follow an extraordinary man like Helmut Maucher. I personally really don't like to hear that 'Someone has followed in someone else's footsteps.' If I were to do that, I would not leave any footsteps of my own.

Peter Brabeck of course does not follow in someone else's footsteps. He makes his own way, but does not distance himself in a nasty way from his predecessor. He evaluates everything he encounters. He did some things differently, sold certain sectors of the company and strengthened others which he thought had potential, and I get the impression that he will also give his successor a free hand.

I noticed the same thing with sponsorship. He minced no words telling me that he would not sign a sponsorship contract that would extend beyond his term as CEO. He didn't want to prejudice his successor. But he was fair enough to put me in contact with his successor, Paul Bulcke, who did sign a new contract continuing the sponsorship. I thank him for that, and I'm sure that Paul Bulcke will have new sponsorship ideas.

In Peter Brabeck you find a combination of staying true to one's roots and being open to the new. There's the saying: "No future without a past." He knows exactly where he's from. He is an Austrian and along with his bond with nature there's tremendous courage – sometimes I would say hubris – pitting himself against the forces of nature. He seeks out extreme environments.

For a long time neither Rainer Gut nor Helmut Maucher approved of that.

I don't think anyone does really. Not even myself, as a friend. He really is a brave person. He has the courage for the non-negotiable business decisions, where courage is needed. In his personal decisions, he has the courage to address certain topics, and make his position clear.

A CEO has to take responsibility for social and political issues. Naturally, profit is the main priority. A company that does not make a profit, that is not economically sound, cannot deal with socio-political issues because it is absorbed in its own problems.

I believe Peter Brabeck has a very precise socio-political compass. He brings accomplishment, rewards for accomplishment, and therefore also money, to those who cannot accomplish things themselves: the very old, the very young, and the infirm.

The subjects of water and the food crisis are very important to him…

I didn't actually know that before. The intensity with which he talks about it is very interesting. After all, you have to be brave enough to deal with making yourself unpopular, and he is.

Peter Brabeck is a person who is confident in himself, not someone who needs his ego stroked on a daily basis. Flatterers get nowhere with him, he does not like that. He acts when he thinks he's right, and in doing so, takes the risk of a conflict.

Because he's a man of action, but also because he is very thoughtful, he gets things moving in the right direction. There are thinkers who hesitate and get nothing done, and there are men of action who think too little under the pressure of action. Brabeck thinks about things for a considerable amount of time, – and his expeditions seem to help him recharge his batteries. He's the type who needs physical challenges to get the energy for the meetings and all the rest.

In summer 2008 we had the Simon Bolivar Youth Orchestra of Venezuela, with the wonderful José Antonio Abreu, as our guests. He founded the youth orchestra in 1975 to give street children emotional support through free music lessons. It's a very moving project. We invited the orchestra, along with its young conductor Gustavo Dudamel, a 27 year old who grew up involved in the project, to Salzburg.

I invited Peter Brabeck to come and see, and I have never seen him so fascinated. He was so happy to see these one hundred young people, gathered in the Festival Hall by their love of music. It was exactly what he expected from the Festival: not freezing up around dignitaries, but passion for excellence. After that, he came a second time, something he had never done before, to hear the orchestra play again.

For a long time I did not know that Peter Brabeck had once wanted to be a conductor. I keep telling industry they should forget their stupid military metaphors; they should look at an orchestra and the conductor. A conductor knows how to make a completely heterogeneous group of voices into a wonderful harmony.

As CEO, Brabeck once brought the Nestlé managers together with an orchestra to highlight the importance of playing together.

Fantastic. That's a wonderful story that shows that he pursues unconventional paths in motivating people. I'm always fascinated by the comparison with conducting. After all, a violin player can't suddenly say that he doesn't feel like playing Schubert today and that he's going to play something else. It's different in a company. Somebody can quietly give up or withdraw, saying to himself or herself, I'll just see what happens.

A musician can't do that; he has to join in; otherwise the project is dead. In the reality of the business world, much is already economically dead, but this is not so easily recognized if some of the actors have become spectators.

Peter Brabeck has an unbelievable vigor and shines like a star when he enters a room. Even in the way he walks. I would never employ anyone who walks slowly. I hate it when people creep along. I know I'm Mrs. Impatience. OK, so I'm impatient, but all my colleagues know it. I have never seen Peter Brabeck look exhausted, not even when he's just back from a long trip.

I always notice when I'm overwhelmed because I start to do things wrong. I'll sit there in a meeting thinking about the next one, and in the next meeting thinking about the one after that, and so I'm not really there out of pure anxiety. I've never seen him like that.

He's also a remarkably good listener. I've only had positive experiences with him, and I get the feeling that he would be a friend in need. I believe he's an immensely loyal person. Loyal to Nestlé, loyal to his colleagues, and loyal to his family. ”

A long road from Villach to Vevey

In December 2008 and again in 2009 the business magazine "Bilanz" chose Peter Brabeck as the most powerful business leader in Switzerland, a distinction which left him rather cold: "Power for me is nothing but a tool to get things done. In this sense power is of course important, because without power, values and principles are laughable."

The judges for "Bilanz" assessed his influence both in his own field and in politics and society. Brabeck, however, only sees his power in terms of the Company. In a wider sense, he has no power, he does not shape the world in Switzerland because he's not a politician.

The Nestlé companies are certainly respected abroad and we stay in close touch with governments and officials in the various countries, Brabeck says. "But I don't think we have any political influence. We don't seek it either; we are neutral in the best sense of the word. We do not serve a government but the people.

"When we invest in a country, we expect three things from the politicians: first, that we have the right to own the company or at least a majority share in it; second, that our intellectual property rights be respected, i.e., patents, trademarks and know-how; and third, that we be allowed to run the company. If people ask my opinion, that is another matter entirely and has nothing to do with power."

Nonetheless Brabeck today ranks as one of the most listened to business leaders in the world. He has received many honors for his work, most recently the 2009 European Business Leaders Award (EBLA) by the CNBC television company.

It was a long way to the summit but Peter Brabeck never asked himself whether or not he would get there – either in the mountains or in his work – for he found the experience of the journey much more important. On that account he never forgot his roots.

He was born on November 13, 1944 in Villach, Carinthia, six months before the end of the Second World War. He spent most of his childhood in number 60 Ossiacherzeile in the so-called "X-Ray Block," the first housing development set up in Villach by the construction cooperative "Heimat" after the War. The apartment was relatively small but it did have a bath and was heated with coal. He was very happy there, he says.

At his school reunion in 2008, 46 years after his graduation, he said that he returns to Villach once or twice a year to visit his mother and close friends. He keeps up his ties in Villach. He has always remained true to his native country, never renouncing his Austrian citizenship, although he was offered Swiss and other passports. He is proud to have contributed to Austria's success and grateful for the good education, values and culture he received there.

In Switzerland he still feels like a guest who respects and likes his host country. He is a member of the local alpine club, his village ski society and the regional flying association; people who don't know he is an Austrian think he is more Swiss than the Swiss. Brabeck loves Switzerland above all because it is so international. There are 80 nationalities working at Nestlé's headquarters in Vevey, and every day he sees how tolerant the Swiss are in their treatment of foreigners.

Peter Brabeck and Austria – Conversation with Wolfgang Schüssel

Wolfgang Schüssel studied economics and law at Vienna University where he obtained a Law degree. He worked first as Secretary of the parliamentary group of the ÖVP and, from 1975 to 1991, as General Secretary of the Austrian Business Federation. From 1979 to 1989, he was a member of the national parliament and, from 1987 to 1989, also Deputy Chairman of his party's parliamentary group.

In 1989, Schüssel became Federal Minister for Economic Affairs and, in 1995, Vice Chancellor, at the same time moving to the Foreign Ministry. From February 4, 2000 to January 11, 2007, he was Federal Chancellor of Austria.

From 1995 to 2007, Schüssel was Federal Chairman of the ÖVP and, from October 1999 until he became Chancellor, Chairman of the party's parliamentary group – a post which he held again from October 2006 to October 2008. He then became a Member of Parliament and foreign affairs spokesman of his party. Since December 2008, he has been President of the non-partisan Association for Foreign Policy and the United Nations.

"I became Minister of Economic Affairs twenty years ago and before that, for 17 years I was General Secretary of the Austrian Business Federation. In both of these roles, and later as Foreign Minister and Federal Chancellor, I naturally got to know Peter Brabeck very well.

As you know, he's from Villach; they are a very characteristic people, shaped by a combination of Romance, Germanic and Slavic culture. Perhaps that also explains the nature of his professional career. It always impressed me that he came from Carinthia, via South America to the summit of Nestlé, an international company. Peter Brabeck is a very attractive human being, a handsome man who is a good speaker and has great powers of persuasion. Above all, he's one of the very few European CEOs whose voice carries weight all over the world. There are many multinational companies where you can't tell who is the top man – Brabeck has never been like that.

Nestlé and Brabeck, it's a special combination. It's probably part of Nestlé's business culture to accept such strong personalities and not to favor gray mice who somehow made their way to the top, but brilliant, scintillating figures; his predecessor Helmut Maucher, whom I know very well, is also an impressive character.

As Federal Chancellor, I meet – twice a year – with expatriate Austrians from the upper ranks of the business world, in which Peter Brabeck also participates. And I must say that his manner and commitment were exemplary. People enjoy listening to him, not because he's important or because of his position, but because he has something to say. His efforts on behalf of an open world economy were very important for us in Austrian politics. And we have lived up to it.

Historically speaking, Austria is not traditionally an export country. Under the Austro-Hungarian monarchy we were responsible for the universities, culture and bureaucracy. It was very important, as Peter Brabeck told us again and again, like an itinerant preacher, you have to broaden your outlook. You can't be self-sufficient, a small country can't withdraw into a shell and be lulled to sleep; you have to go out into the world, use the opportunity of expanding into Central and Eastern Europe and beyond, to Asia.

He also lobbied for getting rid of nonsensical regulations. He always said to us: "Look, we're all in global competition. Founding a company in country X would take three days, but in Austria it would take a year or even 18 months." His recommendations were: get up to speed, be more open, look beyond national borders, make the right investments, not in highways but in "brainpower," new topics and new challenges. Show that you are willing to speak up on the world stage. We have done that consistently, and I think they were very good recommendations.

That's why I can truly say with pride that we have taken Peter Brabeck's message to heart. In the last twenty years we have made gigantic strides in globalization and opening up the Austrian economy. We've quadrupled our exports. Austria has used the opportunities offered by the EU integration, and strongly supported all Austrian businesses – not only the large but also the medium-size – to gain a foothold in all the world markets, from America to Asia, from Africa to the Arab countries.

What I've always liked about Peter Brabeck is that economic success isn't the only thing that's important to him, but he also concentrates on new things. The fact, for example, that he made water a central issue in his social and political agenda. This interested me a great deal because I was defeated several times on this issue as a young Minister of Economic Affairs in the early 1990s. It is appalling that in Central Europe – Germany, Switzerland and Austria – we are using drinking water to wash our dirty cars, water the garden or flush the toilet. We should be able to find an intelligent system that enables the separation of nonpurified water and drinking water.

Initially of course, the idea was ridiculed. Who would finance it for starters? Water, after all, doesn't cost anything and is available in unlimited quantities. But a great deal has happened in the meantime. Due to rising prices for water in industrial production, industry is moving more and more toward the use of ground water, or nonpurified industrial water.

Peter Brabeck's passionate declaration of belief in globalization is perhaps not so popular now during this financial and economic crisis. But we have to remember that globalization has led hundreds of millions of people out of poverty, and that now they might fall back into poverty if we don't act globally to ensure that we come out of this crisis.

Peter Brabeck's plea for a market economy with a sustainable, environmentally-conscious and socio-political sense of responsibility has always impressed me a great deal. Few other European business leaders have the kind of global voice he has. Whether it's in Davos, at UN conferences or advising the American government after 9/11, people listen to him. That's because of the quality of his approach. There are not many CEOs who really think strategically. His main area of concern is: What does the future hold for us? How do we have to prepare ourselves, whether we like it or not? Not: What do we want?

For example, NGOs weren't a topic of discussion 10 or 15 years ago, although there were certain citizens' initiatives in existence which lobbied for or against various things. Today the NGO scene is a seamless extension of government work. That can sometimes be unpleasant, sometimes very hard. The American government under Obama approached this scene deliberately, and it may well have won the election for them. It's the same here in Austria, or in Switzerland and Germany. Today the NGO scene is an important corrective or supplement to politics, especially when they're not trying to stop something, but to change something in a positive direction.

Nestlé is one of the largest of the multinationals at the center of the discussion. The Company has to be able to deal with critical questions, and that's not always easy. Simply brushing the topics away or steamrolling over them doesn't work anymore. I think Peter Brabeck recognized this challenge relatively early and integrated it very well into his actions.

He is a demanding discussion partner. He's someone who will listen when the other person has something to say. But he can be very impatient if someone is just spouting preconceived opinions, clichés or ideological positions. Or, if he thinks someone isn't listening to him with the same openness that he would offer them.

If you want to discuss something with him, you first have to be fearless; second, do not kowtow to authority or tremble in the presence of important world figures; and third, have something to say and be able to present it. Then you will have no problem. I have always found discussions with him very enjoyable – demanding, but always very enriching.

The shareholders are a completely different world. This short-term shareholder mentality, focused on quarterly results, was not around in the same form twelve years ago. Today some shareholder groups are very well organized and aggressive. You have to be able to hold your own against that.

But let's get back to Austria. Peter Brabeck has always had a strong commitment to Austrian culture. The wonderful collaboration with the Salzburg Festival, of which Nestlé is a main sponsor, is due to his initiative. His commitment to quality in the economy and in the arts and, above all, in supporting young people is a fascinating story, and one which Austria has profited from enormously. We are very thankful to him for that.

On November 27, 2006, when I was still Federal Chancellor, I presented Peter Brabeck with the Grand Gold Decoration with Star for meritorious service to the Republic of Austria. It was one of my last duties in office. A few years before, in 2001, he had been awarded the Schumpeter Prize by the Social Democrat Viennese Mayor Michael Häupl. So Peter Brabeck's value is something which transcends party political borders – that demonstrates the quality of his work. ”

Your own ideas are more important than political correctness

"... [Man's] social being determines his consciousness." This saying, which is the core of Karl Marx's dialectical materialism, also applies to Peter Brabeck. That does not mean that he is a Marxist, but that he looks at problems differently from many politicians or business leaders, because of his position in business, politics and society, his contacts, the people he talks to and the information at his disposal. You can indeed see further from the summit; but, and this is one of the prerequisites, you have to interpret what you see correctly.

Globalization has been looked on in a negative light for a long time and as a threat to social peace. In 1996, one year before Brabeck became CEO of Nestlé, a book appeared in Germany entitled "The globalization trap – an attack on democracy and prosperity," which was enthusiastically acclaimed by the media and was seen as a milestone in new thinking.

In two articles which appeared in the "Schweizer Monatshefte" in 2004 and 2008, Brabeck showed that globalization can be regarded quite differently. This liberal periodical, founded in 1921, boasts of its critical debates, courageous writers, outspoken opinions and independent-minded readers. It is therefore an ideal forum for Brabeck.

His 2004 article was headlined: "Globalization: misunderstandings and realities." In it he wrote:

"Seldom has a subject prompted so much misunderstanding and at times even deliberate distortion of facts and developments, as globalization. We hear about developing countries growing ever poorer, homogenized products and businesses which have slipped out of control.

"Admittedly there are problems. Adapting to such a radical change as globalization is bound to have its costs; many people have had to take a slight lowering of expectations which they had taken for granted, but no matter how you look at it, on the whole the effects of globalization are positive. Three points can illustrate this.

"First: affluence is on the increase in industrial countries. People in developing countries are simultaneously more likely to break out of poverty than ever before...Until 1980 the number of people living in absolute poverty was steadily rising. Since the most recent stage of globalization, beginning in 1980, those numbers have clearly declined, in spite of the fact that during this same period we are experiencing the highest population growth ever recorded in history. Once people have escaped from poverty, they do not stand still...

"We have to create better conditions for making the positive effects of globalization felt more quickly and more profoundly, such as the liberalization of agriculture in the industrial countries and the further reduction of subsidies, but also the lowering of trade barriers between developing countries.

"Second: The selection of products is growing. A hundred years ago a working person would find 200 to 300 items in the local store. Today supermarkets offer at least 60,000 products from all over the world and in every conceivable variety... A hundred different varieties of Nescafé are for sale all over the world.

"Third: never before were companies so rigorously controlled as they are today. Globalization means first and foremost globalization of competition. The market transcends borders and spreads into areas where competition had barely existed before... Today we are under increasing competitive pressure, even when it comes to knowledge and the search for key personnel...We saw this several times in recent years: the global market does not prevent mistakes – regulation cannot prevent them either – but it punishes them severely and relentlessly and, thanks to globalization, irrespective of the size of the company. Every year Fortune magazine publishes a list of the 500 largest companies in the USA. Take the 1960 list as a starting point and compare it with subsequent ones, and you will see that in twenty years about a third of the companies have disappeared. Read the 1998 list; the same proportion disappeared in only four years.

"More competition for business is no reason to turn back the clock. This would in any case hardly be possible, for today it is the developing and emerging countries who are promoting globalization as an opportunity for their people."

Brabeck's article in the April 2008 issue was entitled "Why globalization creates variety":

"Local is generally considered to be good, globalization bad. But global – local, I am convinced, are not mutually exclusive but rather sources of reciprocal enrichment and fertility...Correspondingly, the current trend in global markets for food and countless other products is not heading towards standardization but towards a greater variety... This local change, rather than globalization, gives people some serious discomfort...The variety of competition corresponds to the increasing variety in the markets.

"Globalization also enriches culture in the wider sense of the word. To illustrate this point, let us look back at J. S. Bach, who lived for 75 years between Leipzig, Lüneburg and Köthen – a triangle whose sides are barely 250 kilometers long. But his music, which at first glance one might classify as belonging strictly to Germanic culture, was also strongly influenced by contemporary French and Italian musicians. In an early phase Claude Monet painted haystacks in varied light and at different times of the year. His compatriots found them utterly uninteresting but the Americans were enthusiastic about him and bought his works. Without this doorway into the world and greater exposure to new ideas elsewhere, Monet's career might have taken a completely different turn. One final example: African music is looking for new directions; Latin-American music, influenced by Africa, is returning to the African continent in a changed form. Musicians like Bala Tounkara from Mali, play music inspired by Latin America on traditional African instruments like the twelve-string kora.

"Does the same apply to industrial products? Will everyone in the world, under pressure from commercial businesses, eventually only be eating standard six-ounce (170.1 gram) hamburgers?

"Surveys of consumers in Great Britain show that 42 percent prefer local dishes and 62 percent say they want to try something new…

"Add the two figures and they come to more than 100 percent: the desire for local dishes and the desire for new ideas from the global environment are not mutually exclusive. Outside Europe the combination of tradition and openness is even more striking. In China, 74 percent of those questioned want local dishes, while 51 percent want to try something new and in India the figures are 79 and 56 percent.

"Most new foods are generally adapted very quickly to specific local preferences and specific local taste. Take pizza for example. Under the Buitoni brand, Nestlé produces Bella Napoli, a classical pizza made with an original Italian recipe. You can find it within and outside of Europe. When an idea like pizza is established in other countries the recipe changes: Pizza Buitoni's 'Four à Pierre' with chorizo and Emmental cheese in France; Pizza Hawaii with spicy chunks of pineapple in Germany; pizza with chicken and roast garlic in the USA. And if the recipe deviates too much from the original – for instance, with shrimp, mixed spices, roast garlic and three kinds of cheese – a particularly tasty variation from our daughter company Stouffer's in the US – we call it 'flatbread'. (…)

"The most important thing in all this is not to reduce the product to one global average taste. The principle is: everything which the consumer sees, tastes and feels should be local; the rest can be regional or global, all according to what is the most efficient...

"The strong domestic entrepreneurial spirit corresponds to a willingness and ability to operate in a local social context. The role of business is to create value. We make sure that all important social groups in the villages, cities and countries where we are located can participate in the value we are creating...

"We have found an answer – which will continue to be applicable in the years to come – to the reality of the markets, in which the global versus local dimension does not imply mutually exclusive opposites but rather complementary sources of mutual enrichment and cross-pollination."

In these two articles Brabeck broached, in a deliberately unspectacular way, subjects which are nevertheless very volatile. He makes it clear that a Eurocentric viewpoint of worldwide development is no longer adequate to the reality of the situation. Local events and changes are no longer valid yardsticks unless they are also seen in the global context.

Too often we look at our own past through rose colored glasses and think we can simply go along reliving our earlier experiences by the maxim "more of the same." We are too readily prepared to take the existing situation for granted and to close our eyes to the need for further change.

Stereotypical ideas and prejudices prevent us from seeing the real world and the changes that need to be made. The growth of the world's population and the fact that it is becoming younger are not appreciated in a Europe whose citizens are aging and have a latent fear of immigration. No one sees the need to reduce subsidies – they are still seen here as compelling economic necessities.

Many people in the industrial countries are firmly convinced that multinational companies operating globally are out of control, because the state no longer wields control. The role of competition is completely ignored in this context. Peter Brabeck makes it clear that while the market does indeed offer opportunities and freedom, it is also a tough and unyielding instrument of control.

Additionally, globalization offers opportunities for development in the cultural sphere, and it is wrong to insist on a guaranteed existence based on prejudices and false assumptions. As Brabeck proves with palpable examples, globalization does not mean forced conformity, but multiplicity. It is important to abandon traditional thought patterns if we are to recognize how and where new values are being created in the world.

Wellbeing and its importance for the State and for Business

In his speech to the German branch of the International Chamber of Commerce (ICC) in Berlin in May 2008, Peter Brabeck expressed an opinion which is not widely shared even today. The subject of his speech was "The economics of wellbeing: its potential significance for business and economic policy."

Right from the start he made it clear that he could offer neither exhaustive analysis nor conclusive answers but was simply trying an approach which would even deliberately exaggerate a number of things as a basis for discussion. However yet unformed the idea may still be, it nevertheless contains initiatives which will be increasingly significant for business in the future.

When Peter Brabeck saw that the strategic transformation of Nestlé to a focus on nutrition, health and wellness was showing results in real figures, he increased his interest in the concept of wellbeing – not just from an entrepreneurial but also from an economic policy standpoint.

Moves are afoot, for example, to change national accounting methods from Gross National Product per capita to a general index of wellbeing and happiness. Many economists see wellbeing and health as one of the biggest future drivers of growth, and there are initiatives to define wellbeing, happiness and life satisfaction as economic policy targets.

One initiative comes from King Jigme Singye Wangchuck of Bhutan. In 1972, in response to criticism that his country's economy was showing insufficient growth, he ordered that in the future, instead of "Gross National Product," the term "gross national happiness" should be used. According to Peter Brabeck, this concept has in the meantime taken hold in left-wing green groups who, with their post free-market economic theory, want to make significant changes in the social attitudes of businesses.

Even the OECD is looking for alternatives to Gross National Product by trying to find new yardsticks for human wellbeing. Deutsche Bank is trying to record the elements that contribute to satisfaction in the lives of the German people, in which quantitative and qualitative factors, such as trust in others, health, high income, high levels of employment, family and children all play an important part. Viewed from this vantage point it is not Berlin, Frankfurt or Munich which head the list but rather places like Donau-Iller and Ulm.

This way of looking at things could be dismissed as exotic or anecdotal were it not for theories which have examined wellbeing and its future effect on efficiency and growth in the economy. One such theory comes from Leo Nefiodov, a theoretician of the so-called Kondratiev waves. The most recent wave, which is still on-going, is that of information technology, and the next is expected to be a wave that will utilize technological and social innovations to help people to an improved physical and psychological state of wellbeing.

Peter Brabeck's reaction: "Whatever you think of these waves, the basic idea is interesting, namely that we are no longer looking for the equivalent of steam-driven machines (stronger, quicker) in important technological developments; instead what is increasingly important to us is a better understanding and a better fostering of human wellbeing."

Brabeck cites discussions which have given him a broader overview on the subject of wellbeing. He learned from Olaf Blanke, a research neuroscientist at the Federal Institute of Technology in Lausanne, that an increasing number of neuroscientists are studying how to measure and influence general wellbeing – and happiness and satisfaction as part of this – in the brain itself. It is no longer a question of overcoming weaknesses but of promoting and strengthening positive aspects. This will sound to many people like Aldous Huxley's "Brave New World." Brabeck is convinced that individual freedom and decision-making will become even more significant.

Gottfried Dutiné, head of research at Philips, is looking at how sensors in our clothing could record and analyze information about our bodily functions. The possibilities for "smart textiles" are endless: from warning us about an imminent heart attack, to increasing our wellbeing with the aid of heated clothing.

Joachim von Braun of the International Food Policy Research Institute is convinced that wellbeing and happiness in highly developed countries are only possible if life is better for people in developing countries, because genuine lasting happiness cannot exist in the shadow of misery.

Kishore Mahbubani, a social scientist from Singapore, also refers to the societal context. The pride citizens feel in their country, or rather in its technology – China has just taken its first steps into space – demands a sense of wellbeing. The opposite is discontent with one's own country. The black market economy is a measure of this discontent– in Germany it is estimated to be between 17 and 20 percent of Gross National Product. Possibly half of the active population is involved in one way or another with the black market economy.

The experience of community, the playful involvement in a group, the feeling of belonging to someone, to be part of a family are of great significance to the toy manufacturer Alan Hassenfeld. Isolation, on the other hand, creates no sense of wellbeing.

At this point in his report Peter Brabeck makes the link with Nestlé products. Most are aimed at general consumption both by their ingredients and the way they are marketed. The nest as a logo for the Nestlé Company stands for the family and the idea of caring for other people. “We can build on something which was created more than 140 years ago and has proved its lasting worth,” stresses Brabeck.

Prof. Alois Stutzer of Basel University in his research concluded that a consumer’s needs go beyond the simple utility of a product. The consumer wants to know who is behind the product and wants to be treated fairly. For Nestlé this means that prices can’t just be reset by the market situation. Nestlé was able to pass on the high costs of raw materials in the last eighteen months, but this was only possible because in most cases the price increase was associated with an innovation in the product.

When a business is being restructured, according to Brabeck, there should be concern not merely with financial compensation for those affected, but it must be done fairly. These days brands like Nestlé are more than status symbols, they also stand for social responsibility.

He finished his speech with the observation: “The systematic and comprehensive implementation of the concept of wellbeing will influence the standing of the business in society. Here too we must try to understand fundamental trends and not listen primarily to the loudest exponents of political correctness.”

Business must be at the forefront of change

For Peter Brabeck the future cannot simply be derived as a projection of today’s facts; it must be conceived with the aid of new ideas and discoveries. Changes in society are beginning to emerge whose outlines, although still not sharply defined, can be detected in the manifold facets of wellbeing.

Brabeck thinks business has the important task of pioneering such change. This fundamental outlook is also obvious in the “Blueprints for the Future” which he prepared for the Nestlé workforce every eighteen months between 1997 and 2006, in order to communicate his ideas and especially his expectations. He surprised many employees with his blunt analysis of current conditions and his at times radical demands, but also by the personal and emotionally colored form of his presentation.

In his Blueprints Peter Brabeck precisely documents every advance and every setback, and always gives instructions on how the goals under consideration can be reached. His most recent edition ends with these words:

"We don't need to be afraid: a kite only flies against, never with the wind, and yet it doesn't change its place. We are more like a sailboat that goes before the wind and reaches the most distant objectives provided correct decisions are made and faultlessly implemented. We see the right direction in our mind's eye, and all we have to do is be determined to reach our goals."

Brabeck says he always has an opinion of his own and usually expresses it openly. For example, some years ago in Davos he criticized agricultural subsidies, saying that every cow in Europe had the right to travel the world first class with Lufthansa and two cows could take a bull with them for free.

This statement provoked a strong public reaction. People frequently spoke to him about it in person. The then EU Commissioner Franz Fischler came and said that Brabeck didn't understand, that he should realize that agricultural subsidies were necessary. Brabeck replied that he realized this, but that he was trying to prevent the introduction of subsidies which would distort trade. They agreed on this, which was a step ahead, but the conversation would not have happened had Brabeck not given the example of the cows flying first class.

He made a number of other provocative but crucial statements which got discussion going, for example, "No one has yet died of genetically modified products, but they have of bio products," or "Water for the carwash, the washing machine, the lawn or the golf course is not a human right."

Peter Brabeck can also be tolerant of different opinions. The film "We feed the world," for example, presents the subjects of nutrition and globalization in a critical light. The audience is treated to some shocking pictures – ranging from the dreadful conditions in chicken houses, through bread thrown on the dump, to the poverty of Brazilian farmers. Suddenly Peter Brabeck comes on the screen standing in front of pictures of abandoned empty factories saying that everything is fine and we have never had it so good.

Astonishingly enough, he does not mind the way the film portrays him and makes comments about him. He would not take back his words. The fact that the film-maker portrayed Brabeck's statement in such a confrontational way was his right, because ultimately he had to sell the film. "Had I known the context in which the film-maker was going to use my words, I would probably have added two or three conciliatory remarks."

The best information is found on location

Peter Brabeck is critical of the media. What always bothered him, particularly in connection with Latin America, is the discrepancy between real life and its political interpretation by the European media. It made him so skeptical of the media that he no longer watches the TV news because it is too easy to get a false impression, and he does not like to be influenced by television reports. What he wants is an up-to-the-minute analysis of the situation followed by an objective summary.

He only reads a few quality newspapers and takes the time to read between the lines. These include the Neue Zürcher Zeitung, the Financial Times and the Wall Street Journal. Brabeck prefers to form his own picture of situations and has been to Zimbabwe and Pakistan, for example, to see things in situ. He has visited Chinese factories and organized a breakfast with experts – including international journalists, representatives from think-tanks and NGOs – who interpreted the current situation from their own perspective. That experience he found interesting.

If you have the opportunity, the best thing is to talk with the widest possible range of people, says Brabeck. "I have learned from experience that some images give a completely false impression, yet you cannot get them out of your mind." Brabeck is convinced that images can be so powerful that they move your emotions so that you can no longer see the wider, invisible implications. To make decisions you cannot rely solely on emotions.

As an example of this he cites former US President George W. Bush's "axis of evil," the political catchphrase he coined to describe countries that he linked with terrorism. These countries were thereafter shunned. Nestlé takes a different view, stresses Brabeck. It built factories in Syria because it could not stand idly by just because that was the opinion of the Americans. Syria is now one of Nestlé's fastest growing markets.

Nestlé also built three factories in Iran. Admittedly these factories were attacked by an angry crowd as part of a political campaign against foreign businesses but, says Brabeck, the Iranian government stood behind Nestlé.

Meanwhile, a Nestlé North Korea has been founded. Many Nestlé products were already being imported into North Korea from China. An on-the-ground Nestlé delegation found that their products were indeed being sold there, but quality control was lacking, for example, sell-by dates were not observed. Nestlé's first step was to implement quality control.

Multicultural businesses are suited to Switzerland – Conversation with Doris Leuthard

Doris Leuthard, born 1963, studied law at the University of Zurich and, after further studies in Paris and Calgary, was licensed to practice law in 1991. In 1993, she became Superintendent of Schools for the district of Muri and, in 1997, was elected to the Aargau Cantonal Council.

In 1999 she was elected to the Federal Assembly remaining a member until 2006. In 2000, she resigned from her cantonal positions to become Vice President of the Christian Democratic People's Party (CVP), serving as its President from 2004 to 2006.

Since 2006, Doris Leuthard has been a member of the Federal Council, serving as the Head of the Federal Department of Economic Affairs, the central authority for economic affairs and trade policy. Her areas of responsibility include Labor, Professional Training, Technology and Innovation and also the Federal Office for Agriculture, Federal Veterinary Office, and Federal Housing Office. Federal Councillor Leuthard was President of the Confederation for 2010.

“ ***Madame President of the Swiss Confederation, when did you meet Peter Brabeck for the first time?***

It was years ago. There are many events at which members of parliament, i.e. the National Council, sit down with leading representatives of the economic sector. Sooner or later you will meet Peter Brabeck if you are interested in the economy. I was also a guest at Rive-Reine Conferences in Vevey, where you have the opportunity to know people better on both a political and personal level.

Are there any Nestlé activities which you remember with particular clarity?

On my trips abroad I visited many of the Nestlé offices in different countries and talked with the employees and regional politicians. Nestlé was one of the first companies to get a foothold in many of the emerging market nations. So they were on the scene early, investing, creating jobs. People soon thought of them as a local company rather than a foreign investor. That's true, for example, for Brazil as well as China.

On the one hand it makes sense to produce food where it will be consumed and not send it halfway around the world to the consumer. On the other hand, foods often create an affinity with the end customer, to whom it's not that important whether a company is based in Switzerland or elsewhere. In most cases, the consumer sees Nestlé as both a national and a local company, something which the Company lives up to in these countries.

It is different when it comes to premium products, Nespresso for example. For brands like these, linked to such a high demand for quality, the origin is very important. The Nespresso brand fits both Switzerland and our economic strategy.

In a more general sense, to have Nestlé's international headquarters in Switzerland also fits, because with respect to our population, we are one of the most international countries in the world. For decades, we Swiss have lived with many different languages and cultures, and the many multinational companies headquartered here add to Switzerland's international reputation.

Of course, it's also important that these companies show their support for the Swiss ethics and norms, as Nestlé does, by being reliable and credible. My visits to various Nestlé-related farms around the world, showed me that it has a highly developed social competence, hallmarked by sustainability, which Peter Brabeck has always promoted and lived by.

This was acknowledged by the Swiss political world, because it contributes to Switzerland's world-wide image. Nestlé's reputation is very high here at home.

Does Nestlé's good reputation in Switzerland also allow it to influence politics?

Politicians from most of the parties are keen to exchange ideas with Nestlé. To me, that's only natural. But both Peter Brabeck and the Company are clearly reticent when it comes to voting and public discussions, so much so that during the referendum on the free movement of persons we had to encourage Nestlé to address the debate in their company magazine.

That wasn't easy, because it's part of Nestlé's core philosophy not to interfere with Swiss internal affairs. Also on the issue of free trade links with the EU in agriculture, which is of great significance for the whole food industry, we could convince them to abandon their usual restraint. When Nestlé throws caution to the winds by making an exception to the rules for once, this is all the more useful for everyone involved.

Many international socio-economic subjects have benefited from Nestlé's knowledge and practical experience; for example, international rules on competition or the subject of nutrition.

It's nice to know someone who won't intrude uninvited, but who is there with informed opinions and suggestions when needed. It's easy to orient yourself to other countries if you can consult someone with international experience in the relevant area, for example on the issue of water.

Do you ever feel constrained in a particular direction when you get advice from Peter Brabeck?

No. He is a fascinating, excellent and valued discussion partner. It would be foolish not to consult intelligent people. Of course, we don't always share the same opinion. But it's just common sense to get his views and take advantage of his experience.

His commitment to the World Economic Forum in Davos is also part of that, where he contributes his expertise with heart and soul. For example, we had a panel discussion of the respective positions of the USA and Switzerland. I could count on him to ably represent the Swiss position.

In reality, politics and business practice are inextricably linked, each influencing the other. I am thinking of specific regulations which came into force after 9/11.

Are there certain principles and values which Peter Brabeck obviously feels impelled to uphold?
Yes. He's one of those managers who really think long-term. I appreciate that. He lives and breathes the stability of the Company, its finances, investments and profits.

The short-term "quarterly" approach, focused on share values and personal bonuses, is not a priority for him. The components of Nestlé's success are analyzing, anticipating, thinking beyond the horizon.

Prices change, and some raw materials are in short supply. Peter Brabeck's ideas for the future, his long-range investments in new branches of research, new products and markets, meant that the entire Company could continue to operate in relative calm. If you analyze developments and take the time to reassess and make long-term commitments, you can preserve your lead over the competition. That's what I believe is the secret to Nestlé's success.

The second is their eco-social competency. The eco-social market economy is very important for the employees, but also for the many thousands of milk producers and processors. It has always been Nestlé's philosophy to strengthen regional structures within different societies, for example by building up an intelligent milk distribution network. Small farmers were empowered to improve their products, upgrade hygiene standards, and reliably fulfill their contracts. We both gain from this; it's a win-win situation.

Nestlé's philosophy is based on a specific attitude that values human beings. This can be seen in their approach to the environment, such as in coffee cultivation. India, for example, has considerable problems with water shortages, and so it makes sense to create drainage channels where less water is used and none wasted.

I believe a serious and careful handling of scarce resources, which Peter Brabeck promotes based on his eco-social values, is the economic model of the future. Many managers could learn something from him in this regard. In times of crisis, we must hammer away at this message.

Peter Brabeck does not lecture, does not give himself airs nor consider himself as the one and only example for others. But he does show that a company can be successful while remaining true to social and ecological criteria. This message can encourage other companies, and be an example to them. That's to everyone's benefit. ”

"In private I am like everyone else"

In public Peter Brabeck defines himself in terms of his job and his passion, mountaineering. Nothing else in his private life strikes him as worth mentioning and yet he does not object to direct questions, which can help round out his character.

Peter Brabeck is convinced that you cannot receive without giving something in return. He never uses the concept of "making sacrifices." He and his wife Bernadette divorced when after returning to Vevey from South America he was posted back to Venezuela. She stayed in Switzerland with their three children, but they got re-married on his 50th birthday.

Today one of his sons is CFO of Roche in England, the other CEO of Coca-Cola in Finland. His daughter Carolina is a designer and lives near Vevey so he gets to see at least one of his grandchildren regularly. He's less concerned with the amount of time he can spend with his family than with its quality. Every year they all spend a week skiing together.

It is perhaps not surprising that in 2007 he moved from La Tour-de-Peilz (on Lake Geneva close to Vevey) to Verbier where he already had a holiday home and where he now lives in a large chalet. Verbier is a 300 square kilometer sport- and recreation area, particularly for winter sports.

Brabeck is irritated by press reports that his move was a tax dodge, and his denial is credible; there are other places in Switzerland where he could have moved to for that purpose. It seems some people would do anything for money. It was also irritating in 2005, when people said he was seeking the dual mandate at Nestlé just for financial reasons. He considers his earnings of 17.4 million Swiss francs in 2007 to be justified. When he joined Nestlé many years ago, his pay was only 1,500 Swiss francs.

In his time as CEO he increased the market value of Nestlé from 55 billion Swiss francs to 220 billion Swiss francs today, earning 165 billion Swiss francs for Nestlé's shareholders. He patiently answers the question of why he continued to draw 14 million Swiss francs in 2008 when CEO Paul Bulcke earned only 8 million. Until May 1, 2008 Brabeck was performing a dual function and Bulcke was still General Manager. Then starting in 2009, Bulcke's salary as CEO was naturally higher than Brabeck's, who now only holds the post of Chairman of the Board of Directors.

Brabeck agrees with his critics on one point: the Board of Directors' remuneration should be approved by the Shareholders Meeting. He caused some ripples in the media on September 4, 2009, when he pointed out the potential dangers to Switzerland as a business location through wrongful and excessive regulation.

His prime concern regarding the proposed Swiss company law reform, was that the role of the Board of Directors should not be weakened. The introduction of a national salary limit policy was first mentioned – not in a speech – but in an interview with the newspaper "Sonntag," where Brabeck warned against populist-driven legislation, for example concerning bonuses.

Once the public uproar had abated, most leading Swiss politicians agreed with him that regulations should not be overdone. Once again the charge that Brabeck is just protecting his own pocket when he promotes legal guarantees and continuity, and attacks wrongful and excessive regulation, faded.

Money was never his main interest. He says he is not ambitious. He enjoys getting something done, which is a different matter. He enjoys creating and changing things, the way he transformed Nestlé from a food company into a leading nutrition, health and wellness company. That is why he never dwelt much on his career; he just concentrated on the task at hand. "Enjoy your work and you will generally perform a little better than other people."

With that he came back to his favorite theme: "I'd say I like to see myself as a creator. I don't predict the future, I create the future. And I get involved in the big problems such as global water scarcity."

What else is there to report about his private life? His wife's hobby is riding a Harley Davidson, which he has also taken up. She is also a passionate race-car driver; at the track she's a sensation when a delicate-looking grandmother climbs into a racing car and roars off. Brabeck mentions in passing that he is also an enthusiastic glacier pilot.

Besides all these dangerous hobbies, Peter Brabeck regards himself as an epicurean. He once did a blind taste test of six different mineral waters, and recognized them all correctly. Eating is very important to him because he regards it as the ultimate social experience. He eats only Nestlé products, starting at breakfast with a good espresso and a piece of dark chocolate, followed by lunch in the canteen; in the evening he cooks with Maggi or Buitoni products, a hobby for which unfortunately he has little time.

He loves company, but not necessarily big social events. He says that most of his friends are ordinary folk such as climbers, men who run alpine huts and motorcyclists. He was once invited to join the Similaun club but did not do so. The club took its name from the 3,606-meter Similaun mountain in the Tirolean Ötztal Alps, and consists of a group of prominent men led by Reinhold Messner, including Herbert Henzler (ex-head of McKinsey, Germany), Jürgen Schrempp (ex Daimler/Chrysler), Jürgen Weber (Lufthansa), Wolfgang Reitzle (Linde), the publisher Hubert Burda and Klaus Zumwinkel (ex Deutsche Post), who go mountain climbing together. But Messner is not Brabeck's favorite mountaineer.

If he wants to meet important people from the world of economics and politics, he prefers the European Round Table of Industrialists and of course the World Economic Forum, where the world's thousand most important companies are represented. "I have my contacts there," he says.

"Positive, disciplined and independent" – Conversation with Walter B. Kielholz

After studying business management at St. Gallen University, Walter B. Kielholz, born 1951, started his career in 1976 with the General Reinsurance Corporation in Zurich, simultaneously setting up two art galleries with his wife Daphne Kielholz-Pestalozzi. In 1986, he moved to the Schweizerische Kreditanstalt, now Credit Suisse, and, in 1989, to the Swiss reinsurance company Swiss Re in Zurich.

In 1993, Kielholz was appointed to the senior management of Swiss Re and served as its CEO from 1997 to 2002. In 1998 he joined the Board of Directors, becoming Executive Vice-Chairman in 2003, Vice-Chairman in 2007, and Chairman on May 1, 2009.

Since 1999, Kielholz has been a member of the Board of Directors of the Credit Suisse Group and was Chairman of that body from 2003 until the end of his term in 2009.

Kielholz is active in various industrial and economic associations, including the European Financial Roundtable. He is the founder of the Avenir Suisse Foundation, a Swiss think-tank for social and economic development, and was its Chairman until 2009. He is also Chairman of the Zürcher Kunstgesellschaft (Zurich Art Society).

Walter B. Kielholz first met Peter Brabeck in 1999 on the Board of Directors of Credit Suisse Group AG. Brabeck had already been a member since 1997 as Helmut Maucher's successor. What struck Kielholz from the start was the difference in personality between the old and the new head of Nestlé. It wasn't just a question of age but of fundamental personal attitudes.

While Kielholz believes he occasionally saw pietistic features in Helmut Maucher, in Peter Brabeck he sees a man with a positive attitude towards life, a full-blooded manager on the one hand, with a very complex private life on the other. He is completely absorbed in his work as the leader of an enterprise and is the exact opposite of a bureaucrat.

However, as a private individual, Brabeck values challenges and producing results; otherwise he would not be a mountaineer, always pushing himself to the limit, and would not enjoy flying and riding motorcycles. He knows how to get the most out of life. Walter B. Kielholz is one of the few people who can say this because Brabeck is one of his closest friends.

What Kielholz probably admires most about Peter Brabeck is that he has succeeded in leading an independent life not bound by convention on the one hand, and on the other hand has been self-disciplined in serving a somewhat traditional company which he has led from one success to the next. Peter Brabeck clearly manages to reconcile apparent opposites and bring them into harmony.

However, Kielhoz thinks that without Brabeck's South American experience, which he could never have gotten in Europe, his multifaceted personality could never have developed. Combining the experience of rock face climbing, immersion in the South American lifestyle and local business practices is unique.

He compares Nestlé to a sea-going steamer which has to be steered with equal amounts of foresight and sensitivity. Discussions about the dual role may well have affected Peter Brabeck personally but his successes silenced his critics. Clearly he got very many things right, as the numbers demonstrate.

Walter B. Kielholz still remembers Peter Brabeck's support for him when Credit Suisse was undergoing a turnaround in 2002/2003. Brabeck was a member of the Board of Directors from 1997, Vice-Chairman from 2000 to 2005 and again from 2008, and so knows the business very well. The turnaround began in early autumn 2002 and was systematically and consistently continued through 2003.

After posting a loss of 3.3 billion Swiss francs in 2002, the Credit Suisse Group showed a net profit of 5 billion Swiss francs in 2003.

Kielholz also values Peter Brabeck's advice on questions of economic policy, and approves of his reserve and his refusal to get involved in public political discussion. Not to say that he never expresses critical views or discusses controversial issues. Brabeck's strength lay in the fact that he was always well-informed and kept his eye on the facts.

As for globalization, Walter B. Kielholz thinks the close connection between political and business leadership in Switzerland is an advantage. In this context he cited the 1999 founding of the think-tank Avenir Suisse, headed by the sociologist Thomas Held, by thirteen major Swiss companies including Nestlé as well as the annual meetings at Nestlé's Rive-Reine training center.

For a country like Switzerland in particular, it is very important to discuss questions of economic policy on an informal basis, especially if they are of international significance. For large companies like Nestlé, which play a significant role in international markets and have a multicultural leadership structure, Switzerland is of little importance as a production location. It is therefore all the more important that Switzerland, with its multifaceted cultural dimensions should be, and should remain, an attractive location for a head office. The social system in Switzerland and multicultural businesses simply fit well together.

Kielholz says that Peter Brabeck is quite capable of differentiating between exchanging information and cultivating contacts in commercial circles, including the European Round Table of Industrialists and the International Business Council of the World Economic Forum on the one hand, and his personal social circle on the other. In contrast with many other industrial leaders, Brabeck is no socialite; he and his wife are only rarely seen at high society events.

Nevertheless, he is very popular in Switzerland – probably more popular than leaders of the pharmaceutical industry or the banks. Kielholz mentions that he once persuaded Peter Brabeck to appear in formal dress at the Sechseläuten spring festival in Zurich, where he could see his popularity close up.

One factor in Peter Brabeck's popularity, according to Kielholz, is his straightforwardness, for he is completely antithetical to opportunists and people with an exaggerated sense of their own importance. Another factor is that he can discuss the world's major problems, such as the increasing scarcity of water, in easily understood terms. That is more important than being photographed for a story about his home life in a glossy magazine.

Kielholz says Brabeck is rigorous in his handling of information. He is deeply suspicious of popular truths, such as global warming and its consequences, unless all the relevant facts are available and their significance critically analyzed. He tries to avoid precipitous decisions.

Kielholz cannot pigeon-hole Peter Brabeck politically. His views on social matters are varied. Perhaps he is an ecological thinker with conservative values; that would not contradict his defense of sustainability, which is rooted more in business acumen than in ideology.

Some organizations probably need the bogeyman of traditional industry and therefore ignore the trend towards greater sustainability and social justice represented by Peter Brabeck. In these areas too Nestlé is a trendsetter for many other businesses.

Creating Shared Value

The global financial and economic crisis which struck in 2008 continued to dominate public discussion in politics and the media in 2009. It threw a long shadow over other subjects that were equally or more important for the future development of the world.

Peter Brabeck has a pragmatic view of the present situation, saying that we have to live with this crisis and its consequences because the clock can't be turned back. As for the causes and the solutions, his conclusions are quite different from those of the politicians, whose exaggerated activism often forms public opinion.

Peter Brabeck recommends a long-term view, sustainability and solidarity in thinking and acting which goes beyond local, regional or national showmanship. When politicians suddenly rediscover 'the ugly face of turbo-capitalism,' because the employment of their constituents is threatened, they draw a populist caricature of multinationals which often has little to do with reality.

Instead of picking up on the positive efforts of the UN and many multinationals in the Third World and the emerging countries, and making these into a yardstick for action, public opinion in many countries ignores these initiatives. "We cannot grow at the expense of other people," says former UN General Secretary and 2001 Nobel Peace Prize winner, Kofi Annan. That's why creating shared value is so important.

What really set off the financial crisis

Peter Brabeck is convinced that American politicians, not unscrupulous and greedy investment bankers, were primarily responsible for the 2008 financial crisis which turned into a worldwide economic crisis.

With his 1977 Community Reinvestment Act, the Democratic President Jimmy Carter forced the banks to give credit on property to people who lived in neighborhoods which the banks had hitherto considered taboo. President Clinton reinforced this legal obligation in 1995.

The mortgage banks were to give a certain percentage of property loans to disadvantaged groups, especially ethnic minorities and manual laborers, so that even they could realize the American dream of owning their own home. In particular, the state institutions Fannie Mae and Freddie Mac were encouraged to issue generous loans. If anything went wrong, the taxpayer would foot the bill.

So the banks lowered their interest rates and mortgage thresholds. Americans began to invest in their own homes, even people who could not actually afford to do so. In the mid-1990s about 1.2 million new houses were built every year in the USA and, in 2006, 2.1 million, while between 1995 and 1999 interest rates fell from 5.5 percent to 3 percent.

Simultaneously, property prices rose making home buying practically foolproof. In 1999, prices rose by almost 10 percent and a homeowner could calculate that his or her property would double in value in ten years. Sell then, and you will be debt free, and turn a tidy profit.

The risk looked small, so loans were handed out without looking at credit scores. The legal liability of the borrower had nothing to do with earnings or any other personal funds but was simply limited to the house. Anyone who could no longer honor his loan gave the house back to the bank, and that settled the matter.

In 2008, the two mortgage finance companies Fannie Mae and Freddie Mac had outstanding accounts of more than one trillion dollars, fifty percent of which involved low-income borrowers or those without a steady income; by 2007, per capita debt of Americans had increased to 190 percent of their entire disposable income. Mortgages accounted for two-thirds of that debt.

At the height of the property boom, mortgages were being handed out to the tune of more than 600 billion dollars a year, 20 percent of them to borrowers classified as NINJA, which stands for "no income, no job, no assets."

By 2006, the price of homes in the USA began to collapse and it was clear that the system was unstable and about to collapse. Naturally no bank was prepared to carry the risks of these loans alone and so they passed them on. In 2007, almost 60 trillion dollars of credit protection were traded, roughly corresponding to the entire world economic output. What followed in 2008 everybody knows.

Brabeck stresses that a shortsighted, purely political decision more than ten years before, had made a long-term crisis inevitable; but those who had foreseen this were called spoilsports.

Now President Obama's plan intends to spend 75 billion dollars on saving heavily indebted home-buyers from ruin and to rescue their homes from foreclosure, and another 200 billion dollars are earmarked to bail out Fannie Mae and Freddie Mac. Peter Brabeck's view is that Obama is doing the same thing as Clinton years before.

Clinton gave Americans a chance to buy a house which they could not afford and Obama is now helping them to hold onto that house. "Insolvency and foreclosures are causing property values to drop; they harm the local economy and lead to job losses," – that's Obama's reasoning. "We are not just helping homeowners threatened with disaster but also their neighbors who could be dragged down with them." Where this is going to lead in the long term no one knows.

"One of the main reasons we are in this crisis is that in recent years we got more and more used to short-term thinking," says Brabeck. "At Nestlé, we have always seen it as our duty to create value for our shareholders. However, in other companies, shareholder value has more and more replaced sustainable and long-term growth in value, with short-term objectives.

"Years ago Helmut Maucher criticized this and we never went along with it. We never issue quarterly reports, even when pressed by financial analysts. We want to create a healthy and sustainable relationship between shareholder value and stakeholder value with a long-term perspective." Short-term thinking and quarterly results led people in many business sectors to lose sight of substantive goals and concentrate only on short-term benefits. The result: people want it now; they're not interested in tomorrow.

Peter Brabeck is convinced that the business world is not responsible for the present crisis, and therefore the politicians should not regulate the economy. "The idea that business will become more efficient through state regulation is completely wrong."

On September 4, 2009, Industry Day was organized by Economiesuisse (the Swiss Business Federation) in Zurich. Brabeck pointed out the danger that the current company law reform might weaken companies located in Switzerland through erroneous and excessive regulation. The context in which business operates must be kept simple, so that companies can concentrate on productivity. This applies not just to Switzerland, but to the world.

Brabeck added that populism is law in banana republics, but in industrial nations laws should not be changed unpredictably on the basis of opinion polls and short-term political trends. He said: "The crisis has re-opened the discussion about the basis of economic systems. The foundations and achievements of a free society and free enterprise are seriously threatened. Governments believe they have to do everything in their power to increase demand and protect the existing economic structures – regardless of whether they are competitive and sound, or not. This economic crisis is at its core just a symptom of a profound crisis of values."

As a result, the market economy and economic freedom do not rank highly in public opinion at this time. The balance between the state and the economy, between politics and businesses has shifted, to the detriment of the latter. Only a market economy initiative with open and free competition would enable the largest possible number of other people to profit from it. Only with these prerequisites can shared values be created.

Concern about the future

"I can see that in the present situation the state has to intervene quickly," admits Brabeck, "yet I am disturbed and concerned that too much, rather than too little, will be done. Particularly in the USA. If too much help is now given in the wrong place, that could have thoroughly negative consequences in the long run. Naturally it is difficult to find the right balance between what is necessary today and its possible consequences in the future."

Shoring up dying industries artificially by pumping a lot of money into them is not the right decision, he thinks. In the long run, this will mean higher inflation, more subsidies and higher state expenditure, which will mean a growing budget deficit, requiring governments to raise taxes and interest rates. These long-term effects should not be ignored when making short-term decisions.

In just eighteen months, the financial and economic crisis wiped 50 trillion US dollars off the books – almost 10,000 Swiss francs per capita of the world population. According to Brabeck, the greatest losses were suffered by those who had built up billion-dollar assets at a giddy rate rather than the people in highly populated developing countries; he added that now however, the crisis is hitting lower income groups as well. The ILO fears that up to 50 million people will lose their jobs. Of the 2.5 billion people who worked their way up over the poverty threshold for the first time between 1981 and 2005, the crisis could spread and cause 200 million to fall back below the absolute poverty line of 1.25 dollars per person per day at 2005 prices.

This is due not only to the financial crisis but also to the food crisis, of which people in the developed countries are still not aware.

Even the politicians are not conscious of it, nor of the inflation which is coming, says Brabeck.

He pointed out to Jean-Claude Trichet, President of the European Central Bank, and Gordon Brown when he was Prime Minister of Great Britain, that the financial, food and fuel crises should not be taken separately and that the oil crisis was the least important, as it is self-made and only short-term. "We did not leave the Stone Age behind us because there were no more stones, but because we developed beyond it. We shall leave the oil age behind us too, not because there is no more oil but because we have developed a more efficient supply of energy," he says.

According to Brabeck, in spite of all the problems connected with the financial crisis, we should not forget that, in April 2009, the world share index MSCI was still standing at a level six times higher than thirty years previously. First and foremost we have a debt crisis, which we can come to grips with through higher productivity, less protectionism, and structural adaptations.

The food crisis, on the other hand, which is a long-term problem to be taken very seriously, has been aggravated by current political decisions, for example in favor of bio-fuels, seen by many as an important ingredient for solving the climate problem.

Brabeck's view is that we have many more urgent problems in the world than CO_2, which is today at the center of public interest. Even some climate researchers believe that interest in climate change will fade. For Nestlé, there is no higher priority than feeding people. The food crisis is still a largely invisible problem for people in the developed countries, but everyone will become aware of its consequences in the long run if we don't take sustained and appropriate action.

It is important to keep bringing up the food crisis and make clear its close ties to the water crisis. "If we go on like this," concludes Brabeck, "water will run out before oil."

The importance of intangibles – Nestlé Plus

Because of its corporate culture, Nestlé was described by the news magazine "Facts" as a "planet" moving through the business universe according to its own laws, independent of anything else. This picture is not far from the truth. The true reason for Nestlé's success, in Peter Brabeck's view, is neither its market standing nor its financial position, but a phenomenon which internally is called "Nestlé Plus." It cannot be found in the profit and loss accounts nor in the balance sheet, but is something that everyone feels when they have been with the Company for a while.

"Nestlé Plus is about intangible values, the culture of qualitative leadership style, personnel policy and employee relations," says Brabeck. When Henri Nestlé founded the Company, he had a humanistic attitude, he was not just out for success. Because of the high infant mortality at the time, he looked for a product which would save these children's lives and invented Nestlé's infant cereal.

Values still play an important role in the Company leadership, although it has of course been adapted, modernized and refined over the years. Today, Nestlé represents a structure which aims for operational speed with a strong focus on results, reducing bureaucracy as much as possible. Leadership, putting values into practice, and multiculturalism are still the mainstays of the enterprise.

Brabeck is most pleased when he sees the Company's success reflected in the faces of its employees. "That is the best thing; anywhere I go in the world, I see employees looking happy and contented, because they are successful and everyone knows it." They know that they are making a contribution to the whole operation, also on the financial level. Every employee, not just senior management, has the opportunity to earn a bonus and participate in the Company's success. That's why everyone feels a part of the Nestlé success story. "That is the most important thing," Brabeck concludes.

In March 2003, Harvard professors Michael E. Porter and Mark R. Kramer published an article in the "Harvard Business Review", in which they presented to a broad audience their concept of strategic philanthropy. They had found that many companies actually do good things, but that their social involvement is generally unsystematic and serves as a fig leaf.

Governments, activists and the media had become masters in denouncing companies for the social consequences of their business activities. Many organizations ranked companies by their achievements in the field of corporate social responsibility. Although these assessments were often based on dubious methods, they were very popular with the general public.

So, many enterprises did spend a great deal of money on social causes, thereby contributing to improving the environment, but these efforts were nowhere near as productive as they could have been – for two reasons, say Porter and Kramer.

The first is that many CEOs either spend too little money on social causes or spend it in the wrong way, because they regard these outlays as subtracting from their profits. The second reason is that companies often yield to pressure to get involved on a very general social level, even though such involvement has nothing to do with the relevant company strategy. Porter and Kramer conclude that companies are so uncoordinated, working in such isolation from their own line of business and operating strategy, that many of the best opportunities to do something good for society are wasted.

The two professors therefore suggest that managers should apply the same methods to their company's social involvement as those which they use for their core business areas. If they did this, they would soon see that corporate social responsibility can be more than just a cost factor, but that it opens up new opportunities and offers a source of innovation and competitive advantage. Addressing their social involvement strategically can lead to incredible social progress, because their own resources, the know-how and experience of their employees are being used to the best effect.

Peter Brabeck took the two professors at their word and invited them to investigate Nestlé's work in Latin America because that is where Nestlé built its first factory in a developing country, in 1921, and where he had lived and worked as a Nestlé manager for seventeen years, personally experiencing the close connection between social progress and business activities. He said that in Latin America you can see substantial progress, enormous economic upheaval and abject poverty, all at the same time. In spite of that, Nestlé has continued to expand and consolidate its activities, so that today it has 72 facilities there.

Brabeck stresses that, for Nestlé, social responsibility is not something from the outside, but an integral component of its fundamental business strategy and corporate principles, which serve as a "common thread" for all its managers.

He is convinced that as trustee of the shareholders' capital investment he must ensure that the Company benefits society, if it is to make a profit for its investors in the long term. The real test of a company is whether it will benefit society over the long term; this is why Nestlé commissioned the Foundation Strategy Group, of which Mark Kramer is Managing Director, to analyze how Nestlé puts its social responsibility into practice. Nestlé also asked for recommendations on how to more closely harmonize the relevant activities with overall Company strategy.

Furthermore, the Group was to collect information on the influence exerted by Nestlé on the social fabric of Latin America in recent decades. The results of this report would then be the basis for creating shared value worldwide. Nestlé managers gave the researchers access to important information, supported by internal documents and interviews.

The investigations proved that Nestlé has a profound, positive influence on the people and their environment in Latin America; the findings were published in 2006 in a comprehensive report entitled "The Nestlé concept of social responsibility and its application in Latin America."

Nestlé's next step was to submit a report on Creating Shared Value which was published along with the Company's 2007 Annual Report and the report on Corporate Governance. Using Michael Porter's "Value Chain," it documented the creation of shared value at each stage of the chain.

The first link in the chain – agriculture and rural development – was based on know-how and support for farmers, as well as making current research and development available to suppliers. Nestlé's Creating Shared Value concept consists of ensuring a supply of high-quality raw materials and improving relations with society as much as product quality. The creation of value for society consists in improved yield and higher income, together with reduced exploitation of natural resources.

The next link in the value creation chain embraced the effects on the environment, production and employees, based on investment in local production facilities. The advantage to Nestlé is lower production and distribution costs; the advantage to society is the creation of employment in rural communities.

The third link concerns products and consumers, based on building up brands by responsible marketing and increasing the value and volume of sales. Nestlé's advantage is entry into new and emerging markets as well as achieving a competitive dividend for shareholders. The value created for society consists of broader access to foods that are preferred by the consumer, and the generation of local investment and economic growth.

In the report on Creating Shared Value, Peter Brabeck concludes that Nestlé is respected worldwide, and especially in developing countries, as an enterprise which fulfills its responsibility to society to a large degree. He adds: "We are not content with the status quo. … this report is a first step on the road to preparing worldwide data on creating shared value."

Building on Kramer and Porter's ideas, Nestlé has produced a plan covering several years which should facilitate an increased and more comprehensive assessment of creating shared value. By using the GLOBE management information system, it is possible to give access to global information on Nestlé in many areas for the first time.

Insiders are convinced that Nestlé would not have been so successful with the principle of Creating Shared Value if Brabeck had not demanded and sponsored a complete revision of the R&D division. Today Nestlé has a much broader base than when it was just dealing with basic food technology. Unlike the traditional food industry, today it has innovation pipelines such as in the pharmaceutical industry, with technology platforms previously only to be found in high-tech industry.

The plant biotechnology used by Nestlé today, which provides farmers in Third World countries with millions of healthy plant seedlings and thus guarantees the survival of the agricultural sector, has not been developed by any other enterprise in the world. Today Nestlé has a gene bank for cocoa and coffee plants which protects them from extinction caused by new pathogens.

Through cloning plants by embryogenesis it was possible, for example in China, to work with local farmers and create such a large coffee-growing area to ensure sufficient raw materials for the first Nestlé coffee factory in the country. This model, which has since been transferred to other countries, goes far beyond the principle of sustainability as developed by Brabeck's predecessor, Helmut Maucher.

The reasoning was simple: industry cannot produce good products if it does not have high-quality raw materials at its disposal. And so Maucher founded an Environmental Advisory Committee in 1990. But Nestlé's concern is much broader than merely operating in a healthy environment. Today its agronomy expertise is transferred by its 800-plus assistants to farmers all over the world. It was Peter Brabeck who blended the idea of sustainable and environmentally friendly action with Creating Shared Value.

Stimulating thinking instead of off-the-shelf solutions – Conversation with Amir Dossal

In 1985, after more than fifteen years in leading positions in various companies, Amir Dossal moved to the UN, where he led several new initiatives. As Executive Director of the United Nations Office for Partnerships, he is today the UN representative for Public Private Partnerships.

His responsibilities include the United Nations Fund for International Partnerships, money from which has so far financed more than 450 programs and projects in the fields of child health, women and population, climate change and biodiversity. In 2005, the UN Democracy Fund was set up with the task of strengthening democratic structures and supporting governments in new or reconstituted democracies.

In 2006, Dossal set up the first Peace-Building Support Office, to help countries which had suffered conflicts overcome gaps in their development. In 2007, he created an economic advisory board to contribute to the reinforcing of foreign investment in the fields of energy, environment, transport and tourism in North East Asia.

“ *When did you meet Peter Brabeck-Letmathe for the first time?*
We met for the first time about four or five years ago. Nestlé was in discussions with the then Secretary General Kofi Annan on how best it could support the work of the United Nations, in particular the Millennium Development Goals. He asked us for concrete ideas to help Nestlé put their commitment to Corporate Social Responsibility into practice. In my first encounter with Peter, it became quite clear that he was a dynamic leader and passionate about making a difference to humanity.

Are there any joint activities or projects you remember with exceptional pleasure?

Nestlé is a truly global brand and under Peter's leadership they remain committed to engaging its staff and Nestlé products to support the achievement of the Millenium Development Goals (MDG). We advise Nestlé from a strategic perspective on how to address some of these issues and challenges. For instance, we are looking at ways for Nestlé to use their product labels to send positive messages about achieving the MDG, and highlight issues of prevention and better healthy lifestyles.

For instance, Nestlé is doing excellent work in helping farmers in Africa, where they are training farmers to produce better quality dairy products, with a consequential improvement in their earning capacity. At the same time, Nestlé benefits because they can improve the quality of their end products, which in turn could help them reduce product recalls. It is thus a win-win for the farmers in Africa and for Nestlé. This is the concept of creating shared value. In 2009 Nestlé hosted a meeting in New York – the first of its kind, where this concept was introduced as a universal corporate target.

What do you expect for the future vis-à-vis Creating Shared Value?

We think that this model is the new corporate culture amongst a number of companies, although they may not have identified it as the shared value concept. Prof. Porter had highlighted this some years ago, that this should be embedded in all companies. Creating a better understanding that it is not just a one-way-street, but a platform where everyone brings expertise and experience to the table, and we must benefit from each other's comparative advantages. By working together, we can create a more humane and responsive society.

Do you see any concrete effects from the Creating Shared Value meeting?

I think it is a combined issue. After that meeting, several companies expressed keen interest in adopting this concept internally. Some companies are already practicing this, while others are exploring how to put this into concrete action. What we are seeing is that this concept is in its early days, and an attitude shift is taking place which is urgently needed in this current economic climate.

Peter Brabeck stands by his commitment to make Nestlé into a socially responsible and open global organization. He is a strong voice for the industry, and Nestlé being one of the largest conglomerates in the world can make a difference by engaging its peers in the food and beverage industry. I think this is Peter's unique leadership.

Peter is a highly respected person not only in his field but as a global citizen. He is able to broaden the concept and not necessarily push it as a Nestlé issue but as a shared value initiative, which can be embraced by all. He gets it – he is able to do good, and do it well at the same time. We cannot simply think of the bottom line alone, we must think of how we are making a difference in the lives of others, particularly the underprivileged.

How do you see the relationship between Nestlé and the NGOs? Apparently Nestlé had some problems with NGOs ten years ago, and Peter Brabeck tried to find a solution?

I know breast milk substitutes is an important issue for Nestlé, and we are equally sensitive that this needs to be addressed. The primary concern relates to marketing of breast milk substitutes. Organizations like UNICEF and WHO are quite concerned about the marketing issue and insist that the first thing we must promote is mothers' milk. UNICEF recognizes that in the event mothers' milk is not available, substitutes could be used.

And some of the NGOs are very adamant and say that when companies aggressively sell and market milk powder, it takes away the opportunity for the mother to breastfeed the child. That has been the biggest issue; an agreement regarding marketing has been made, but not everyone in the industry has accepted it.

UNICEF has asked us to bring together some of the companies who manufacture breast milk substitutes (BMS) to see how they can adopt norms and guidelines on advertising and marketing of these products while also promoting the importance of breast milk. I don't think there are any issues today between UNICEF and Nestlé.

The WHO International Code of Marketing of Breastmilk Substitutes goes back to 1982. It is an important code, since it provides concrete suggestions on how to handle this issue, and how companies should advertise and market BMS. The importance of breast milk is paramount, and where it is not available, or not healthy for the child, substitutes can be used. We are encouraging Nestlé to work with UNICEF and WHO to collaborate on this issue, and to bring the industry together.

We can't however overlook that this topic is a contentious one for some civil rights activists, and that the NGOs therefore take a rigid standpoint. The NGOs think that companies are only focused on making money, while companies like Nestlé say that they are considering both sides: 'We perfectly understand that the health of the mother and child comes first, and we are not marketing just for the sake of marketing.' The World Health Organization's Code of Conduct addresses how to objectively inform the mother about the importance of breast feeding.

The industry needs to adopt a stringent advertising code which includes prohibiting the use of photographs depicting happy babies on cans of milk. The code also restricts distribution of free product samples.

Peter Brabeck is a kind of pioneer for change in this area. In fact if you look at Nestlé's website, you will find quite a bit on this topic.

You have said that Peter Brabeck is a strong proponent of the Millennium Development Goals. Do you have some examples?
We feel that not only must you act, but you must also encourage others to act. Captains of industry have an important role, to highlight the challenges and offer people ideas for change without necessarily promoting their own models. Peter is a fine example of this effort. The biggest challenge in any environment is not to say that you have all the answers and therefore all the solutions. You need to hear from others too.

His attitude has been that we should figure out how we can make a difference by working together. And that's what Peter has been proposing – that the MDG is a responsibility of all citizens. He has been a valuable and respected voice on this subject and often talks about the MDG. Under his leadership, Nestlé has not just been focused on the core aspects of their business, it is also using its global reach to find solutions for basic needs; an example of this is Peter's commitment to the CEO Water Mandate.

It is not easy for me to campaign on this matter. The voice of someone like Peter is more listened to, since it is heard in the context of concrete action. He can offer concrete solutions, not only how Nestlé is making a difference but also how others can contribute to achieving the Millennium Development Goals.

Is there anything important which should not be missed in this book? The title of the book is Creating Shared Value and this issue is the leitmotif for this book. It shows a complete picture of the person and his work, and a view of the future.
This is very important, this is the key thing. He is not sitting on his laurels. His voice is a clarion call. He does not say he has

the answers but rather offers a few ideas you can consider, and then use to make a difference. Everyone should develop their own model, based on their own lifestyle or business, and then act! That's a very important point. We cannot preach to people about how they should do things; we can encourage them to be more creative themselves.

Peter is a cut above the rest when it comes to drawing the best out of people. Others often have a tendency to say 'I have the solution, I have the answers, follow my example.' Peter Brabeck doesn't say that. He says, this is the way we do it, but others are also doing good work, and they may have a better idea than we do, so why not collaborate, why not learn from each other's experience and expertise? And that is what really makes Peter so different, I think. He is a true global citizen and a humanist, and a model for others. We need many Peter Brabecks if we want to create a better world. ”

The importance of Creating Shared Value for Nestlé

On April 27 and 28, 2009, in partnership with the UN Office for Partnerships and the Swiss Mission to the UN, Nestlé held a Forum on Creating Shared Value in New York. Top Nestlé managers consulted with internationally acknowledged experts in the fields of business strategy, water, nutrition and rural development. Also participating were the thirteen members of the newly-founded Nestlé Advisory Board for Creating Shared Value. This advisory board, says Brabeck, would analyze the Nestlé value creation chain and suggest possible measures for promoting Creating Shared Value, in order to reinforce the positive effects on society against the background of the successful development of a business.

At the Forum, three initiatives were introduced underlining the Company's involvement in Creating Shared Value. The first is the "Nestlé Healthy Kids Global Program." Nestlé anticipates launching nutrition and sports programs in twice as many countries as currently by 2011, so that more than one hundred such projects will be started in countries where the Company is active. Issues include malnourishment and increasing obesity, especially among schoolchildren. Currently Nestlé supports educational programs which reach over ten million children.

The second initiative – opening an R&D center in Abidjan, the largest city of Côte d'Ivoire – underlines Nestlé's commitment to the development of rural Africa. This center is to help improve agricultural productivity and ensure the West African food supply through its new research programs for developing and improving agricultural products such as cassava, maize, coffee and cocoa, as well as cereals.

The third initiative is the Nestlé Prize for Creating Shared Value. Every two years, awards of up to 500,000 Swiss francs are given to individuals, NGOs or small businesses that come up with innovative solutions to malnutrition, access to clean water or progress in rural development.

Since half of all Nestlé factories and employees are in developing countries, it should come as no surprise that about 2.4 million people earn their living in Nestlé's supply chain. In 2008 Nestlé made 27 million dollars in small loans available to about 600,000 farmers worldwide, to help them conquer poverty, become better suppliers and boost their economic potential.

Brabeck believes the current financial crisis once again proves the truth of the following economic principle: "If you fail to work on behalf of the public interest, and take shortcuts that place the public at risk, you will also fail your shareholders. We believe that to have long-term business success you must simultaneously create value for shareholders and for the public. In Nestlé we call this Creating Shared Value and regard it as a core principle in running our business."

At the Creating Shared Value Forum in New York on April 28, 2009, Brabeck gave the following closing address:

"First I would like to tell you how and why we arrived at the subject of Creating Shared Value. It all began at the 2005 meeting of the

World Economic Forum in Davos. Many of you will remember it, because the meeting had made quite a splash because of the stars who had been invited to attend.

"During that meeting, Corporate Social Responsibility (CSR) became perhaps the most important subject. After only a short time it developed its own dynamic, as often happens at such meetings, everyone began to agree that we have to give something back to society. Then Sharon Stone stood up, and within two minutes she had managed to collect something like a million dollars by appealing to the guilty consciences of my fellow businessmen.

"I took no part in this, but at the end I stood up and said: 'As you know, I do not believe that I have to give something back to society, because I haven't stolen anything from it; I am convinced that through our business activities I have already created value for society.'

"This ended the final session of the 2005 World Economic Forum. On the one hand, raising a million dollars made a good impression, and it would certainly be put to good use, but on the other hand, I do not think that this is the right road for Corporate Social Responsibility. It is very limited and there were several interesting reactions to it. The "Wall Street Journal" said that bad business leaders should not have the right to put shareholders' money into charitable causes; we also got some violent reactions, for instance at our investor road shows. But several of our major shareholders inquired whether we were involved in charitable causes and what we are doing within the CSR framework.

"The Davos meeting had significant consequences and compelled me to think over the role of our Company in society. It is clear that you can't run a business without a society to run it in. Therefore, our responsibility, besides to our shareholders and investors, is also towards society. We are responsible to both: the shareholders and society.

"So, how we conduct our business became vitally important. That's when we began discussions with Michael Porter and Mark Kramer, who had invented the concept of Creating Shared Value. We wanted to try it out, because this concept contained both the idea of CSR and the business leadership that would correspond to it.

"When we look at our business activities, our first and foremost concern is to abide by the laws and regulations of each country in which we operate. Sustainability is at the top of our value creation chain, because our enterprise should endure for the next 140 years, not just the past 140. And sustainability can only be at the top of the value creation chain if it is grounded in the concept of Creating Shared Value.

"Once we recognized that, and after working with Michael Porter and Mark Kramer for three years, we asked them to look at Latin America, to see whether we really are creating shared value and sharing it locally over the long-term.

"It took three years for us to bring our concept of Creating Shared Value to this Forum. I think that by itself shows that this is not a short-term activity for us or that we want to attract attention. It is a long-term obligation for our enterprise, by which I mean that we are talking about a period of ten to twenty years, not one, two or three years.

"We invested three years to arrive at the point we are today. This long-term obligation to Creating Shared Value is to become a part of our Company culture and everyday decision-making for our 283,000 employees worldwide. This is particularly important, because within Nestlé we also value decentralized decision-making very highly. Only by embedding the concept of Creating Shared Value within our culture can it be lived on a daily basis.

"That is how and why we came to the Creating Shared Value concept and why we are so keen on it. Another aspect is how we set our priorities. As a leader in the field of nutrition, health and wellness, we did not focus so much on the multiple connections between economy and society, but food stood out as one of the main pillars of our business. Of course water was also important, because it is closely tied to sustainability and inseparable from the subject of wellness. Wellness cannot exist without clean water.

"Thirdly our relationship with over 600,000 farmers in rural areas is very important. The development of rural areas, where you find the most abject poverty in the world, is particularly important. It is a field in which we can be active, as part of our business activities and not merely as something extracurricular. We are on site every day in these areas. Nutrition, water and rural development are thus closely connected, which will have multiplier effects that will go far beyond today's Forum.

"One of the most difficult steps for private enterprise is to also influence political processes and decisions. But I assume that those attending this Forum have the experience and enough credibility to do so appropriately.

"What we wanted at this Forum was to make clear the role of the economy in Creating Shared Value and to draw attention to the three important subjects of nutrition, water and rural development. I think we have succeeded."

Nestlé has proved that together everyone can win – Conversation with Michael E. Porter

Michael Eugene Porter, born in 1947, studied space technology and mechanical engineering at Princeton University and got his PhD. in Business Economics from Harvard. At the early age of 26, he was appointed Professor of Economics at the Harvard Business School and, in 1971, he took over the leadership of the newly created Institute for Strategy and Competitiveness. Michael Porter is one of the world's leading economists in the field of strategic management. He has become well known for his work on the subject of strategy and competitiveness. He advises many leading American and international businesses on competitive strategies and is also consultant to a number of foreign governments.

"*When did you first meet Peter Brabeck, and what is your relationship with him today?*
I met him about five years ago. In the course of conversations and meetings to discuss Nestlé I have gotten to know him well, and consider him one of the truly pioneering thinkers and actors in forging a positive role for the corporation in society.

What are the problems and mistakes of the companies in their efforts to improve the social and environmental consequences of their activities?
The primary mistake that companies make is to think of social and environmental consequences as a cost or constraint on their operations, rather than as a new opportunity to reinforce their strategy and further differentiate themselves from competitors. Companies also tend to separate their Corporate Social Responsibility (CSR) activities from their core business, treating them as a matter of public relations or reputation rather than as a substantive part of their business. As a result, companies focus on the limiting negative impacts of their operations, and miss the opportunity to add a social dimension to their commitment to value and improve their competitive position by improving social relationships.

Are there "Creating Shared Value" activities or projects of Nestlé which could be a model for other companies?
There are many. The company's core strategy of continual optimization by upgrading nutritional value and reducing fat content, while maintaining their commitment to taste for the consumers, is itself an excellent example of shared value creation. This improves the company's competitive position while also improving the health of its customers. Nestlé also creates specialized food products that meet the nutritional needs of specific groups, such as undernourished children or the elderly.

Nestlé has numerous Shared Value Initiatives in developing countries around the world in the coffee, cocoa, and dairy farming sectors, including China, India, Africa, and Latin America.

To take just one example, the Nespresso division has created shared value in coffee growing areas through enhanced procurement practices involving local coffee farmers.

Nespresso concluded that obtaining coffee through traditional channels would not ensure a steady supply of the specialized and high quality coffees that it requires. As a result, the company began working directly with farmers and regional co-ops to create shared value that would benefit the farmers as well as the Nespresso division.

Nestlé worked in partnership with the NGO Rainforest Alliance to teach farmers more sustainable farming practices, and partnered with local farmer cooperatives to implement a farm productivity improvement program. Nestlé also provided new seedlings, along with pesticides and fertilizers, that together dramatically increased crop yield. Nestlé agronomists also identified the highest performing farms and documented their results so that other farmers could follow those examples. The company helped cooperatives create shared wet mill facilities and provided test grinders to check the quality of the coffee at the point of purchase, enabling the company to offer a higher quality coffee at the point of sale. The company benefits from a more sustainable higher quality supply of specialized coffees for Nespresso, and the farmers benefit through higher incomes and improved livelihoods for themselves and their families. The community benefits from less environmental impact.

Do you see new opportunities for Nestlé to put Creating Shared Value into practice?

Nestlé has only recently begun to fully connect all its core business operations across the entire company with the opportunities to create shared value. As this integrated approach to corporate strategy and corporate responsibility becomes more deeply ingrained in management at all levels of the company, many new opportunities are likely to emerge to create shared value at local and regional levels. The company will also be able over time to better align more of its traditional CSR and philanthropic expenditures with its opportunities to create shared value.

How do you evaluate the role of public pressure on a company to do good?

Public pressure on companies has both constructive and destructive components. On the positive side, most companies, even those that are leaders in creating shared value today, first woke up to the social consequences of their business activities as a result of public pressures from activist organizations. This pressure forced companies to confront the social dimensions of their businesses and their supply chains in ways they had previously overlooked.

However, there are at least two negative sides of public pressure. First, the general public isn't always accurately informed about every social issue or about the company's true behaviors. Targeting global corporations as wrongdoers has proven to be an effective fundraising technique for nonprofits, but it is often unfair and excessive. It sometimes hampers efforts by companies that are actually the most innovative. Second, public criticism has often led companies to focus on the appearance of creating shared value through public relations campaigns and sustainability reports, rather than the reality of shared value through core business activities.

Overall, if NGOs practiced shared value thinking rather than confrontation, they would be more effective and companies would do much more good.

How do you see the role of Nestlé in the global economy and global society, and the part of Peter Brabeck-Letmathe?
Nestlé is among the leaders in connecting the economy and society through providing economic opportunities to small-hold farmers and factory workers around the world, through innovations in technology, and through the nutritional value of its products that feed billions.

As a company that operates with a long-term vision and a 30-year strategic plan, Nestlé understands the importance of integrity and trust versus short-term opportunism. Nestlé has emerged as a leading model of sound corporate citizenship

Peter Brabeck has personally been at the forefront of many important social issues, such as access to clean water, as well as the entire creating shared value movement. He has brought these issues to the attention of the global business community through his leadership at the World Business Council for Sustainable Development and the World Economic Forum at Davos, among other forums.

He has also championed the concept of creating shared value, supporting the development of major research projects, advisory boards, and international gatherings to focus attention on the idea. Peter's vision of business as a positive contributor to society has helped reshape the field of corporate responsibility, moving beyond the focus on the harm caused by businesses to the opportunities businesses bring to improve lives of people around the world. ”

Credibility only comes through concrete action

"We must give something back to society." Peter Brabeck reacts with mild irritation to this phrase. He often had to listen to this in the past, without ever getting the impression that the person uttering it knew what he or she was talking about. Repeating such slogans, which somehow sound positive, must be some kind of herd instinct.

"What should I give back to society?" says Brabeck, annoyed. "I have neither stolen nor taken anything from society and it has given nothing to me. As a successful business, we give many people employment which they urgently need and we pay them better than other employers, including fringe benefits. We also pay our suppliers better and are often the only ones to buy their products at a decent price. We process raw materials to supply our customers, and do so as efficiently and environmentally friendly as possible, using the least possible resources. A business's only fundamental duty towards society is to create jobs and to produce useful products in a sensible way."

However, says Peter Brabeck, something is hiding behind this expression "giving something back to society." Particularly in Europe, many entrepreneurs are put on the defensive and are increasingly influenced by the purple prose of their PR advisers. Unfortunately they often don't think about what they are actually saying. "Many people say we need to win back trust and credibility, and hope to do this through more rules on corporate governance and so-called corporate social responsibility. But rules that stay on paper do not generate trust," Brabeck says.

You gain credibility through concrete action. Openness, honesty and straightforwardness, clarity of thought and word, the ability to act effectively are the core competencies of an enterprise, which must be understood and lived daily.

Charity as practiced in the USA may seem right and sensible for individuals, but financing charitable projects is not the task of managers, because ultimately they are not giving away their own money but that of the shareholders. Only money spent on projects which contribute to the common good and represent sensible business investments, can be justified.

On the subject of shareholder value, Brabeck stresses that many Nestlé shares are owned by pension funds that secure members' pensions through investment in the Company, so that there is a direct connection between providing for the old age of many pensioners and the success of the business.

Another thoughtless cliché used equally often is the concept of "fair trade," which implies that all other forms of exchange of goods must be unfair in principle. As with the idea of having to give something back, the underlying assumption here is that businesses are generally exploitative and basically do harm to society. This cliché also obscures the necessity and significance of free trade.

The market economy is often seen as a zero-sum or even a minus-sum game, where there always has to be a winner and a loser. Many people cannot possibly imagine that business activities can turn everyone in a society into winners.

Whoever thinks of this in terms of taxes paid by corporations has only grasped part of the picture. Businesses serve to create value, in other words to increase assets, not to diminish them, says Brabeck. In this context there is another concept which scares many people – competition. Brabeck is convinced that "more and more intensive competition was and is one of the major sources of widespread, sustainable increase of prosperity for us and worldwide." Nevertheless fear of competition is increasing and people become suspicious when you speak about competitiveness.

Remaining competitive means working constantly by individual efforts, flexibility in business, and reforms at both the national and an international level. That simply means changing, improving and adapting to new circumstances. With this in mind, you can see why not everyone can or wants to be competitive, and therefore many people will experience change as painful.

Competition is in general seen as a threat to jobs, to personal status and prosperity. Rather than this, people should see competition, and the greater differentiation (including in pay and performance) that comes with it, as a way to encourage people to take more responsibility for themselves and for shaping their future. Competitiveness begins in the mind of each individual. That simply means creating qualitative growth by changing current conditions and enabling the realization of new ideas and innovations, Brabeck stresses.

This skepticism about competition as a fundamental principle of the market economy is particularly vehement in Europe. The European Round Table of Industrialists (ERT), in which Peter Brabeck is also active, is a forum of forty-seven corporate heads of major European industrial and technology companies, drawn from a wide spectrum of fields spread across eighteen countries. Their total turnover comes to about 1,600 billion euros and they employ about 4.5 million people worldwide. The key aim of the ERT is to promote the competitiveness of European industry.

Brabeck considers the ERT a very important European institution. Its task, amongst other things, is to defend European competitiveness and it must therefore play a constructive political role. "Whether or not we are always successful is another matter," concedes Brabeck.

"I probably talk less about that, because I always have the feeling that we would only be really successful if European competitiveness were to increase significantly, but I don't think it is increasing. I think that Europe and European enterprises need a different self-conception and a different self-image if they are to remain competitive in the long term."

"We cannot grow at the expense of others" – Conversation with Kofi Annan

Kofi Annan was born in Ghana in 1938 when the country was still a British colony. In 1958, he started a course in economics in his hometown of Kumasi and then transferred to Macalester College in St. Paul, Minnesota, graduating in 1961. He subsequently studied at the Institut Universitaire de Hautes Etudes Internationales in Geneva and, in 1972, as a Sloan Fellow he graduated with a Master's degree in Business Administration from the School of Management at the Massachusetts Institute of Technology.

In 1962, he started working at the World Health Organization of the United Nations. Between 1974 and 1976, he was Director of Tourism in Ghana and then returned to the United Nations to work in various positions as Assistant Secretary General. In 1994, he became Under Secretary General for Peacekeeping Operations, interrupting his job for five months to act as the Secretary General's Special Representative to the former Yugoslavia.

On January 1, 1997, Kofi Annan became UN Secretary General and, on June 29, 2001, he was appointed for a second five-year term to the end of 2006. In 2001, he was jointly awarded the Nobel Peace Prize with the United Nations.

In 2007, he founded the Kofi Annan Foundation to continue playing an active role. The three main aims of the Foundation are to raise public awareness of vital global issues and to promote constructive solutions to them; to make a tangible contribution to peacekeeping through advice and mediation, and to support other organizations in their work.

For this reason, Annan took over the chairmanship of the Alliance for a Green Revolution in Africa, an initiative which began in 2006 with funds from the Bill & Melinda Gates Foundation and the Rockefeller Foundation. Its aim was to double or triple agricultural production in Africa over the next ten to twenty years. Kofi Annan is also one of the founding members of the Global Elders, a group of outstanding figures who want to play a part in solving global problems through their influence and experience. He is also Chairman of the high profile Africa Progress Panel.

" ***When did you meet Peter Brabeck the first time and how would you describe your relationship to him today?***

I first met him at the World Economic Forum late in the nineties. I could see he was someone who had a modern approach to management issues. He was an open person and had easy contact with people. This quality is extremely important for leaders, managers and politicians because it often boils down to recognizing people's problems early and solving them. Sociable people like Peter Brabeck are good business leaders. Since I first met him, he has moved up the career ladder, and I am not surprised that he's made it to the top.

How would you describe your relationship today?
We have regular contact because we are both on the board of the World Economic Forum, and we both attend the board meetings. We also sometimes meet at social gatherings and if there is an issue we need to discuss we can call each other and discuss it. As you know, I was the one who set up the Global Compact and he was one of the early supporters of the concept and the whole concept of social responsibility. Nestlé was one of the early companies that joined the Global Compact; you know I suspect a lot of it was due to its own ethos.

Are there any other companies that joined the Global Compact as early as Nestlé?
There were others, but Nestlé was definitely one of the early ones. I think the first year or two we had about 200 companies joining and Nestlé was definitely among them; it has maintained its interest and deepened its commitment to social responsibility. Nestlé has made the Global Compact into a key component of its business principles.

Did the other companies do the same as Nestlé, and include the concept in their corporate principles?
Some did, some only agreed and some put it as part of their corporate principles and included this in their annual reports. I think Henkel and Deutsche Bank did so, but Nestlé was one of the early ones.

Are there any joint activities or projects with Peter Brabeck you remember with exceptional pleasure?

Not projects, but there was a time that there was a misunderstanding between Nestlé and UNICEF. I recall a meeting between Brabeck and the Executive Director of UNICEF, Carol Bellamy. And I think they were able to think through their differences in a way that allowed them to cooperate in the future. I had arranged the meeting between the two sides, as I had done with Maucher before.

Do you think there is a chance that the concept of creating shared value will be generally accepted?

Yes, I think we have no choice but to accept it. We live in a world where the only way we can prosper is to work together. We are in the same boat. One cannot prosper at the expense of the other. One cannot be secure at the expense of the other. And particularly when you look at climate change. You cannot be prosperous if you don't take responsibility for the environment and nature. If you are not sensitive to the society in which you live and from which you make your profits, you are not going to be successful in the long term.

I often say that a company should not need national legislation to understand that they cannot pollute the village drinking water. A company should not need national legislation to understand that it has to pay a decent salary to the workers. A company should not need legislation to understand that it should use the earth's resources in a sustainable way. Because sometimes we exploit the resources of the world as if there were no tomorrow and there were no children coming up. I think the way Nestlé and some companies are thinking about social responsibility is the way to go.

Which other companies?
There are other companies that are trying, I think some in the same industry, Unilever, I mentioned Deutsche Bank, in fact we also set up another group called Responsible Investment and we had quite a lot of Wall Street companies sign on.

In most of the countries where Nestlé is producing and selling its products, the company is governed by national standards of nutrition. What is the role of Nestlé with regard to international criteria, and what part does Mr. Brabeck play in this?
Of course Nestlé is a big international corporation and as you say different countries have different laws which have to be respected, but at the same time there are minimum international standards that all these companies have to respect. Particularly when you sign on to the Global Compact, you need to be careful to be seen as responsible and correct in your dealings. As a national company you honor the national laws, you operate in a manner that ensures the development of the country in which you are operating and wherever possible you subcontract to local suppliers, giving them a chance to develop and grow.

I think Nestlé is one of the companies that has been very active in this area. Obviously when we set up the Global Compact, we saw this as voluntary but also transparent. Some NGOs were unhappy and said it has to be a law, it has to be imposed. But the UN cannot force that sort of thing. Transparency is a very powerful tool; if a big company adopts it, and claims to be doing something, and the employees say it is not, then the transparent approach is a very powerful way of keeping everybody honest. You don't always have to impose something on institutions or people. But some NGOs would not appreciate that.

How has the relationship between Nestlé and the NGOs changed over time, and what was Peter Brabeck's role in this process? What do you think about the importance of the NGOs in the future?

I cannot answer the first part of your question but I suspect being the sort of open-minded person that he is, he has probably given greater access to the NGOs. And let me also say that the NGOs have a very important role to play in almost every country today, and there is a dynamic or perhaps even a robust NGO community developing. They are organized, they are alert, they are able to keep the politicians on their toes, and play an important role in society.

And I think we are going to see continued growth of NGOs, not only in developed countries but also in the developing world. Now they are all linking up into an international movement which can be very effective. Without the strong support of the NGOs for example, we could not have banned landmines. We also had very strong support from the NGOs in establishing the International Criminal Court.

What part will Nestlé play in the future development of global society?

I think companies like Nestlé have a very important role to play, not only today but in the future. We all remember the food crisis last year and the prices going up. Today we are about six billion people in the world and we are having trouble feeding them; by 2050 we will have nine billion. How are we going to feed them? So research in processing and food handling like Nestlé is doing is going to become even more important.

Food manufacturers have to be innovative; they have to be creative and work with producers and farmers to ensure that we have enough to feed the ever growing numbers of people on our planet. I am sure leaders like Peter Brabeck are aware of this challenge.

Nestlé held a Creating Shared Value meeting in April in New York, together with the UN, and announced a Shared Value Award. What is the reaction of the governments and other companies?
I must say I don't know enough about the Shared Value Award. Shared Value I think is very important and I will say that communities are held together by shared values whether in one country or at a regional level. We need shared values and in my discussions with companies and governments they have all accepted this idea. Social responsibility is supported by many governments. Some governments have realized long ago that government cannot do everything and that with Corporate Public Partnerships you can get a lot done.

Is there anything important about Peter Brabeck which should not be missed in our book?
I think you can say that he is a very modern man, a man who has broad horizons. From a very young age he worked in other countries and realized that we all live in the same world. He is sensitive to other cultures and this makes it easier for him to approach people. He is an example of what a modern manager should be in the sense that in today's world you cannot think in purely local terms. What you do in Switzerland or Germany has an impact on other countries and what they do has an impact on you. And so every leader, every manager has to think in much broader terms. I think this is something that comes almost naturally to Peter. ”

Nestlé's road to a transparent company

Since the late 1960s, no other multinational has been criticized more severely than Nestlé by such a wide range of stakeholders. To this day accusations made over the decades seemed to have become prejudices etched in people's minds. On top of that, the issue was often not even a question of actual or alleged wrongdoing, but the way the Company handled criticism and the critics.

An insider put it like this: "The bigger a company, the more firmly it is believed that all problems can be solved from the inside. Yet one thing cannot be changed from the inside, and that is the external perception of the company. Only a very high degree of transparency can help in this." It was probably the case that the relationship between Nestlé and its stakeholders really was characterized by a total lack of understanding. That only changed when Peter Brabeck made the nine principles of the UN Global Compact an integral part of Nestlé's own corporate principles.

The Global Compact is a value-oriented platform which was proposed by Kofi Annan in 1999 during the World Economic Forum in Davos. It now comprises over 5,000 businesses, together with organizations representing employees, human rights, and environmental and development issues throughout the world. As Kofi Annan set them out in 2001, the principles first and foremost provide a basis for focused dialogue on learning and exchanging experiences about what works and what does not.

Peter Brabeck decided to have this dialogue with the relevant people, i.e. the people in the developing countries who work with Nestlé as employees, suppliers and partners or are active in local communities. Nestlé's 2003 Annual Report for the first time ever recorded its involvement in the UN Global Compact.

In 2007, Nestlé organized the first official meeting with external stakeholders to get concrete feedback on the strategy of Creating Shared Value and on various essential subjects. Meanwhile, implementation of the Global Compact principles and the Millennium Development Goals of the United Nations is now included in Nestlé's annual report.

As early as 2005 Nestlé introduced a company-wide audit program in which three leading international independent certification bodies examined compliance with local laws and with Nestlé's own business principles. The name of this program, CARE, stands for Compliance Assessment of Human Resources, Safety & Health, Environment and Business Integrity. Today, with its self-imposed standards and their external verification, Nestlé has gone far beyond anything ever demanded by its stakeholders.

Peter Brabeck's next mission

"My vision is that we will one day have a health service and a Health Ministry that lives up to its name; in other words, that it does all it can to ensure that people stay healthy and don't become ill in the first place," says Peter Brabeck. "In my opinion, in the Western world at the moment we only have an illness service and an Illness Ministry, because today's medicine, important as it is for people, is simply a repair shop for curing illnesses."

In the OECD countries, the proportion of expenditure on preventive medicine in 2004 was a mere three percent of total health expenditures, which was clearly too little. Experts are convinced that the growing prosperity in industrial and emerging countries will, in the next few years, lead to a dramatic increase in chronic illnesses. PricewaterhouseCoopers concludes that, by 2015, about three percent of global economic output will go into curing "prosperity illnesses" such as diabetes, heart and circulatory diseases, and back pain, if preventive health programs are not significantly stepped up.

In 2005, chronic illnesses accounted for approximately 60 percent of all deaths worldwide and we can assume that, by 2015, the number of people dying from heart disease, cancer or other chronic illnesses will rise by 17 percent from 35 to 41 million. At the same time the number of deaths from infectious illnesses, malnutrition and inadequate medical care will fall by 3 percent.

Since people are living longer today than ever before, and the proportion of older people in West European countries is going to increase steadily, the logical consequence is that the incidence of chronic illness will increase sharply. Although obesity is not officially included as an illness, serious obesity, technically known as adiposity, represents a growing problem for mankind. The WHO speaks of it as "the scourge of the 21st century" and warns of a collapse of health services. The WHO estimates there are about one billion overweight people worldwide, of whom 300 million suffer from adiposity.

In today's world there are more people overweight than undernourished. By the WHO's reckoning every other person in the USA is overweight. In Germany, almost 50 percent of women and 60 percent of men are overweight and the proportion of overweight children has risen by 50 percent over the past 20 years. About 1.9 million Germans between the ages of 3 and 17 are overweight and 800,000 suffer from adiposity. Of the 75 million children and young people living in the EU, 22 million, about 30 percent, are overweight and 5 million are adipose. Obesity is not only limited to the USA and Europe; it is also a problem in Australia and in the Middle East, in some Pacific islands and increasingly in emerging countries such as China and India, where a marked increase in the number of overweight people is forecast for the coming years. By 2015, China will incur economic costs (in figures adjusted for purchasing power) of US $ 550, Russia US $ 300, and India more than US $ 200 billion on chronic diseases, including treatment costs, absence from work and related expenses.

Because of tight public health service budgets – and probably also due to the lack of political insight – an increasing number of major businesses have decided to take preventive action themselves in the interests of the health of their employees. Nestlé not only offers balanced menus in its lunchrooms and cafeterias but also provides special health programs for its employees in many locations around the world. A fitness center was opened underneath the cafeteria in the Vevey head office.

The central role of nutrition

Nestlé sees nutrition as the most important factor for health because good health cannot exist without proper nutrition. On the one hand, nutrition has to address the question of people who are undernourished and suffer from chronic hunger, and on the other, proper nutrition for the population of the industrialized countries.

A mineral and protein deficiency seriously affects both the mental and physical development of children in particular. Malnutrition causes a number of deficiency symptoms and illnesses which can often be fatal. It is estimated that 24,000 people worldwide die every day as a result of malnutrition, 13,700 of whom are children.

Nestlé's goal is to make food of high nutritional content available at low prices to poorer people in developing and emerging countries. The long established selection of "popularly positioned products" (PPP) is constantly expanding, while the most modern nutritional and food technologies help produce safe, nutritious products at affordable prices. There are currently more than 300 PPP initiatives in 70 countries.

It is important that these products reach consumers even in the most remote regions; Nestlé has organized its own distribution networks in several Asian and South American countries to supply products directly to small local traders who then take the goods into the rural areas by delivery van or motorbike. In other countries, middlemen are used to sell the products either to local mom-and-pop stores or directly to consumers at weekly markets, community centers or other social gathering places.

A large proportion of the population in these countries suffers from a lack of important micronutrients such as iron, zinc, iodine and vitamin A. By enriching the PPP with low-cost nutritional supplements, Nestlé contributes towards alleviating the most serious deficiencies. Since many people cannot afford meat, fish, poultry or eggs, Nestlé's research team is constantly working on the development of milk-based products which can be stored without refrigeration, milk being naturally calcium-rich and a good carrier of nutritional supplements.

In Argentina, Bangladesh, Chile, Morocco, Pakistan, South Africa, Singapore, Colombia, Algeria and the Pacific Islands, low-cost enriched milk products have been specially developed to provide energy, protein and micronutrients needed by growing children. Their brand names are Nido, Nespray, Kim, Gloria and Sunshine.

Nestlé has the largest privately-owned food and beverages research program in the world and is the world leader in offering dietary solutions. In 2008, almost 2 billion Swiss francs were invested in its 26 R&D and Technology food and drink centers, and in its extensive external collaboration network. These facilities throughout the world serve to gear the Nestlé products to local nutritional requirements and to suit local tastes. In China, for example, in addition to the existing R&D center in Shanghai, a new center was recently created in Beijing, where over one hundred scientists and technicians research the potential health benefits of traditional Chinese ingredients.

Nestlé aims to develop and offer high-value food and drinks which are beneficial to the health, and have added nutritional value. Moreover, everything must appeal to the consumer, which means existing products are constantly being checked and new ones developed. Ingredients such as salt and fat, which can be harmful in large amounts, are reduced.

Lack of micronutrients is widespread in industrialized countries as well as in developing and emerging countries and consumers' nutritional deficiencies vary from country to country. While these deficiencies can in principle affect anybody, the risk is particularly high for the elderly. Today up to 50 percent of residents in nursing homes and up to 70 percent of older patients in hospitals are malnourished, which incurs even higher care costs than adiposity. Nestlé has developed food supplements for this target group and also a diagnostic device which recognizes existing or imminent malnutrition.

These products belong to Nestlé Nutrition's Healthcare Nutrition division, which also works on products for people with particular illnesses such as cancer, and for children with gastro-intestinal diseases; for artificial feeding by stomach tube there is a replacement food high in fiber but cholesterol free. With the acquisition of the medical nutrition division of Novartis at the end of 2006, Nestlé took a significant step forward in the market for medical nutrition to second place internationally after the US pharmaceutical company Abbott.

Other business divisions in Nestlé Nutrition are baby food (strengthened in 2007 by the acquisition of Gerber's baby food business from Novartis), performance products for athletes and other active people who are aiming for top-class physical and mental performance, and weight management.

In 1981, Nestlé introduced low-calorie instant meals onto the market under the brand name Lean Cuisine and, in 2006, Nestlé Nutrition acquired Jenny Craig. This new business area offers a tailor-made weight management program, in other words, not just calorie- and portion-controlled products but also an individual exercise program and personal advice on an integrated healthy lifestyle from 3,500 experts in 700 centers.

"The fact that we are repositioning ourselves as a health business is not primarily an ethical decision but more a commercial one," Peter Brabeck admits. "I see the subject of health as one of the most crucial waves of innovation in the food industry." In the previous forty years, convenience was the driving force behind Creating Shared Value and in the next twenty years major value creation will come from products with added health benefits. The long-term strategy is quite clear to Brabeck: "We have to move to personalized nutrition and, through it, to personalized preventive health programs." In order to build this up, improved diagnostic technology will be required because today it is generally acknowledged that there is a connection between human genetic make-up, nutrition and health.

For example, in societies where the population gets 90 percent of its energy requirement in the form of carbohydrates such as rice or cereals, a Mediterranean diet based on 30 percent fat, 30 percent carbohydrate and 30 percent protein is quite wrong. Such a diet would not necessarily suit the Japanese and it would certainly not suit the indigenous people of polar regions who get more than 90 percent of their energy from fat.

What applies to the population as a whole generally applies to individuals as well, according to Brabeck. A person with a lactose allergy, for example, needs a different form of nutrition from someone with other allergies or weight problems.

We still have no comprehensive picture of the interaction between genes, illnesses and specific foods. Genetic tests currently being offered by some US businesses, cannot give a person's status, let alone prescribe the best nutrition for each case. For that, the complete genome and metabolism would have to be mapped. That's still years away.

Brabeck's image of the future is sharply defined: "By 2050, we will have personalized nutrition. We will use individual diagnostics to turn nutrition into a preventive health factor." By that time Nestlé will offer personalized menus for cancer prevention, for example, and personalized diet plans and products for a range of other health issues.

In spite of this complex interplay, we must not forget that one of the main preconditions for a healthy life is access to clean drinking water and to adequate basic nutrition. This closes the circle. There will be no healthy nutrition if we don't solve the global water problem.

Is there a future for a Wellbeing Company?

When in 1974, under its French Chairman Pierre Liotard-Vogt, Nestlé bought shares in L'Oréal, the price tag was 260 million Swiss francs. Today those shares are worth about 22 billion Swiss francs. Nevertheless, Nestlé would be in a position to buy out the Bettencourt family shares because the stepwise sale of the ophthalmic specialist Alcon to Novartis brought in approximately 39 billion Swiss francs.

A merger of L'Oréal and Nestlé would create a huge firm with a turnover of more than 130 billion Swiss francs and 340,000 employees worldwide. But there will be no quick decision, because this is not operational, but strategic. Time to reflect can only be to the good.

The contract between Nestlé, which holds about 30 percent of the L'Oréal shares, and the Bettencourt family, which holds 31 percent, provides that neither party can increase its holding until six months after the death of Liliane Bettencourt. However, since April 29, 2009, both sides have been free to sell their shares in the cosmetics business. Financial analysts and the media have speculated intensively about whether Nestlé would separate from L'Oréal and sell its shares. The two firms collaborate in two joint ventures – Galderma for the treatment of skin diseases and Innéov, which produces nutritional supplements "for beauty from within." Brabeck reports that Nestlé took 18 months to decide not to sell and to continue its participation beyond April 29, 2009.

The Nestlé Board of Directors asked Peter Brabeck to think about Nestlé's future with L'Oréal. Brabeck thinks the real issue is not whether or not to sell the shares; it is a strategic decision: what will be Nestlé's next move?

Almost ten years ago Brabeck drafted his concept for a nutrition, health and wellness company. It was later decided not to go ahead with the pharmaceutical arm that had been mooted in the draft. The question is, might it now be possible to create a wellbeing company. Would it have a future? If the answer is yes, this would become Nestlé's next "gap creation." Brabeck is still working on the answer. Every six months he briefs all the members of the Board of Directors on the progress of his thinking.

If Brabeck and the Board of Directors conclude that there is no chance of "gap creation" with a wellbeing company, it would be pointless to hold onto L'Oréal over the long term.

If, on the other hand, a wellbeing company is seen as the right long-term strategy, a merger or closer cooperation with L'Oréal might make sense – but that is only one of several pathways, Brabeck stresses. "I'm sure it's not the only one." But the first question is strategic, to decide on a Wellbeing Company. "On that, we still have some work to do."

Acknowledgments

Looking back over the year spent in preparation for this book, including research, interviews and writing, I realize that the credit for the success of this undertaking is only partly my own. Many other people whose names are not to be found in either the title or text, have made their indispensable contribution.

First and foremost I would like to thank Peter Brabeck-Letmathe, who gave this book its substance and its liveliness, spending many hours patiently talking and answering questions; he put material from his personal archive at my disposal, encouraged, corrected, and wrote down his personal memories, impressions and thoughts.

Nor could I have written this book without the many interviewees, who gave up some of their valuable time to shed a true light on Peter Brabeck's work and his person from different angles.

Kofi Annan, Nobel Peace Prize winner and former UN Secretary General, and Amir Dossal, Executive Director of the United Nations Office for Partnerships, threw light on the globally significant aspects of Peter Brabeck and Nestlé's international collaboration with committees and institutions. The same applies to Professor Klaus Schwab, founder and president of the World Economic Forum, who gave me special insight into Peter Brabeck's thoughts and actions which revealed some new aspects to the reader.

I also thank Professor Schwab for his spontaneous agreement to write the foreword.

Helmut Maucher, Honorary Chairman of Nestlé, and Rainer E. Gut, Honorary Chairman of the Credit Suisse Group, threw light – as only insiders can – on the complex relations between the Company, the personality and the multifarious demands made on the people at the top. Helmut Maucher's perceptive analysis combined with true feeling, helped me to see and understand things more clearly, not just for this book.

Doris Leuthard, Swiss Federal Council member and President of the Confederation in 2010, Fritz Gerber, Honorary Chairman of the Zurich Insurance Company (now Zurich Financial Services) and Hoffmann La Roche (now Roche Holding), and Walter Kielholz, Chairman of the Swiss Re Board of Directors, enabled me to put Peter Brabeck and Nestlé's influence into the political and economic context of Switzerland, and they all also contributed to my understanding of aspects of Peter Brabeck's personality.

Dr. Helga Rabl-Stadler, President of the Salzburg Festival and Dr. Wolfgang Schüssel, former Federal Chancellor of Austria, gave me quite a different angle on Peter Brabeck, showing me his artistic side and his ties to his homeland.

I have to thank the colleagues of my interviewees – Peter Frey, Susanne Helmsley, Jacqueline Hess, Lucie Hrbkova, Yvonne Jaeger, Katharina Lindsberger, Natalie McDonnell, Esther Rentsch, Sabine Schiessl and Doris Weckmann – for making these conversations possible.

At Nestlé, Rudolf Ramsauer and Anne-Marie Guarnero kept tabs on everything and gave me all the support I needed, aided by Albert Pfiffner of the historical archives, Herbert Oberhänsli, and many other employees whose names I wish I knew.

Werner Bauer, Executive Vice President of Nestlé, must get specific mention, because he showed me the importance of R&D in Nestlé's success.

I especially want to thank former press spokesman François-Xavier Perroud, who retired in 2008, for his organizational loyalty, and for being there when I needed help for over a decade.

I thank the publisher Manfred Hiefner, the project leader Martina Frei, and the editor Esther Hürlimann, who supported me wholeheartedly in making a presentable book out of a manuscript.

Of course I thank my wife Ruth who has shared in the work, as she does with all my books. She rarely steps into the limelight but everyone involved knows of her inestimable contribution.

Finally, I want to mention two people who have nothing to do directly with this book: Maria and Harry Krause from Kronenburg. They looked after our cats and freed my wife and me to conduct our interviews and travel in Switzerland and elsewhere in Europe, without a care.